D0575816

The 25 Days of Christmas

The 25 Days of Christmas

An Advent Celebration for the Entire Family

REBECCA HAYFORD BAUER

VICTOR BOOKS

A Division of Scripture Press Publications Inc.

Most Scripture in this book has been paraphrased by the author. Specific quotes are from *The New King James Version* (NKJV). © 1979, 1980, 1982, Thomas Nelson, Inc., Publishers; and *The Living Bible* (TLB), © 1971, Tyndale House Publishers, Wheaton IL 60189. Used by permission.

Copyediting: Barbara Williams
Cover Design: Paul Higdon; Tim Botts
Cover Illustration: Rebecca Hayford Bauer
Back Cover Photo: Brian Aveni

ISBN: 1-56476-517-6

Suggested Subject Headings: ADVENT; DEVOTIONS

Recommended Dewey Decimal Classification: 242.33

2 3 4 5 6 7 8 9 10 Printing / Year 98 97 96 95

Contents

Acknowledgments

I can never adequately thank all of those who helped me bring this book to completion. Here is just a small token:

To Stephen and Audrey LaVaggi—Your "creative instigation" worked! Thank you for the watercolors and for being Santa's Elves.

To Brenda Josee—Thank you for your encouragement and help in refining the project to its final form. This wouldn't have happened without you.

To Rob Dunkin, florist extraordinaire—Thank you for your many suggestions and hints on how to decorate a Christmas tree.

To Diana Acuña, Lana Duim, Debra Goldstone, and Gunta Irbe—Thank you for your continuous prayer support. I felt it every step of the way.

To Michelle Glush—Thank you for taking the time to give me "art hints."

To Cindy Henderson—Thank you for your prayer, your support, your friendship, your lunch times(!), and your incredible gifts as typesetter and graphic designer.

To the staff at Victor Books, especially Dave Horton, Barb Williams, Paul Higdon, and Andrea Boven—Thank you for advancing this project through to its conclusion! You're all wonderful!

To Mom and Dad—Thank you for helping me learn how to celebrate Christmas joyously in the first place!

To Brian, Kyle, and Lindsey, the three most awesome kids in the world—Thank you for learning how to cook, clean, and do laundry this year! I love you.

And to Scott,
my wonderful husband, who's been making
my dreams come true for 20 years—
Thank you for believing in this one.

Introduction

Christmas is a joyous, bright, heartwarming, miraculous season. It is a time to dwell on the miracle of Christ's birth and delight in the warmth of family. However, Christmas is also a hustling, bustling time of year, and as a young mother, I found that my tendency was to hustle and bustle my children off . . . to their rooms, to Grandma's, outside—anywhere but where I was so that I could take care of the profusion of additional chores that accompany the season. There were other things to juggle at Christmas too—school, soccer, carpool, even having to cook every night! Things that normally fit comfortably into our daily lives became major projects in December. But in my diligence to accomplish all of these responsibilities, I had completely missed the point! This was a time for us to work together, to play together, to celebrate and laugh together.

Christmas has long been called a season for children. But I had become so involved in the busyness that the children were set aside. I found myself so busy with doing things *for* them (buying gifts, planning surprises) that I wasn't spending time *with* them in giving, in baking, in decorating, in wrapping. And in teaching them about the miracle of Christmas.

My story has a happy ending! As I stepped away from the "urgent" and took a good look at the "important," I realized that what I really wanted was to give my children their first taste of what Jesus' coming really meant. I wanted to be the one who explained to them the story of salvation incorporated within the Christmas celebration. I wanted them to begin to understand the eons of time that had passed since God had promised Adam and Eve that the seed of the woman would come to bruise the serpent's head and He would redeem us back to Himself. I wanted them to get a grasp of the centuries under a law that no one could possibly fulfill; the darkness and futility of a life without God's continuous presence. And I wanted them to sense the joy of that first Christmas when into this world of sin, darkness, and futility burst the Son of God, the Light of the world, the Redeemer, God with us . . . Jesus.

Yet these things cannot merely be spoken. They have to be lived and breathed. One way to do that is to fill every Christmastime with so much joy and meaning that it becomes a natural part of a child's life, because it is a natural part of our family!

For many people life in Jesus and joy are mutually exclusive. "Joy" is suspect because life in the love of God is reduced to rules and spiritless service. But "joy to the world" was God's idea. He said that spirituality and joy were supposed to go together! Scripture tells us that we are to "serve the Lord with joy and gladness of heart" (Deut. 28:47), that His joy will fill us with strength to accomplish what He has set before us (Neh. 8:10), and that "in His presence is fullness of joy" (Ps. 16:11).

For me, the blending of these two aspects of Christmas are best summed up in a song:

Holy Homes

Jack W. Hayford

Hang the lights, come and string the berries,
Make another ornament to trim the tree.
Have a bite of a chocolate cherry,
Pour another cup of Mamma's Christmas tea.
Candles, holly, creche, and angels,
Bells, and balls, and mistletoe.
Holy homes needn't be unmerry,
Jesus and His coming fill our hearts with glee.

Buy a goose, plan a feast that's dandy,
Bake a dozen pies and make the pudding plum.
Candied yams, buttered rolls, and chutney
Overflow the table with the best "yum-yums."
Sugar cookies, brandied fruitcakes,
Sticks of peppermint and gum.
Holy homes filled with bowls of candy,
Honoring the sweetest Babe that e're did come.

Come and kneel now, beside the tree now,
Let us open presents we have wrapped in love.
But while kneeling, a holy feeling,
Overflows our hearts with praise to God above.
His the gift that makes our Christmas,
Jesus, Savior of mankind.
Holy homes know He's made us free now,
Free to live in life, and free to live in love.

As you ask the Lord to fill your home with holiness *and* happiness this Christmas, may this book help you to make a spiritual, practical, and emotional investment into the lives God has entrusted to your care.

Foreword

I'm smiling as I write—big-time smiling!

I'm about as joyous as Christmastime makes me, but it isn't even near that lovely season as I'm inscribing these words.

Still I'm "tickled," as we often say—but it would be more appropriate to say, "Tickled red-'n'-green" rather than "pink," because this is an introduction to a marvelously creative book about "Christmasing."

Please meet *one happy handbook* and also *one wonderful woman*. They are the reasons behind my smile and my being "tickled," because I've been asked to introduce them to you. Let's take the lady first.

Rebecca Bauer, whose creative genius and flair for turning the most imaginative idea into something practical anyone can do, is the author of this book. She's also my daughter, and that's probably the primary reason I'm smiling, because I'm one proud dad.

I'm not only proud because she's done such a fine piece of work in this extremely useful, family enriching book. I'm particularly thankful for the vision and the values that undergird her producing what I think you'll find to be a timeless resource for making Christmas lovelier than ever at your house.

Becki (her "grew-up-with" name) is a busy, devoted wife of a pastor who serves a demandingly large congregation, as well as an efficient, loving mother of three—including two teenage sons and a 10-year-old daughter.

What you have in hand is the work of a woman whose motivation is to build a healthy, happy, and holy environment into all the life of her family. And she *does* this. As you read, you'll find this wife-and-mother's vision applied to just one season, but believe me when I say—"She lives and serves these values *all* the time."

Woven into the fabric of these pages is more than merely bright, joyous ideas for celebrating Christmas in the true spirit of our dear Savior's coming. There are character-building concepts and life-deepening hints that will bring dimension as well as brightness to this precious season. Which is to begin my introduction of the book too.

Here is one happy handbook designed to take the "weary" out of Christmastime's fuller-than-average schedule. I predict it's going to add new quantities of the genuine joy intended in the original Christmas to your heart, your home, and your family.

The Twenty-Five Days of Christmas is the overflow of the heart and hands of a young woman who grew up in a home where Christmas was celebrated with unabashed fun as well as undiluted meaning. As she and her husband have established their own home, they've carried this tradition to new and brighter levels of joy and happiness. And that makes me all the happier.

Christmastime was meant to bring us love—at every level; from creating the most boisterous, festive laughter and enjoyment to answering our hearts' most deeply whispered prayers. Here's a helpful guidebook; a format for a faith-filled as well as a fun-filled Christmastime observance. It's new evidence that every generation can find not only the happiness and excitement of Christmas, but can do so while keeping sensitive to its meaning and message.

Jack W. Hayford
The Church On The Way
Van Nuys, CA

How To Use This Book

Dear Parent,

This book was written with the intention that it would grow with your family over a series of years; that it would be a servant to your family . . . not a hard taskmaster. In other words, don't feel obligated to do everything in the book, every year!

Perhaps one year you'll want to focus on the devotionals for the Sundays of Advent. Maybe another year you'll want to learn all the verses to some Christmas carols. Choose several activities that will enhance your family life *this* year, and leave the others for another time.

The 25 Days of Christmas has four distinct features for you to tailor to your family's needs and personality. As you do, may this be a memorable Christmas filled with the joy of Jesus and the fun of the festivities!

Feature 1 A series of **daily devotionals** to *equip parents* to communicate their faith to their children and grandchildren through the story and symbols of the Christmas miracle, AND to *provide children* with the recognition that God has a plan for their lives that He will personally reveal to them.

Feature 2 **Worship music**, via hymns and Christmas carols, that will add to the joy in any home, reinforce the lessons learned, and plant eternal truths in children's hearts.

Feature 3 **Hints to parents** on how to incorporate their children into the Christmas planning and activities, and to offer ideas of things to do with their children to make Christmas fun.

Feature 4 **A Christmas check list** gives a practical guide for holiday preparations, helping any family to move through the Christmas season with joy and anticipation—stress-free!

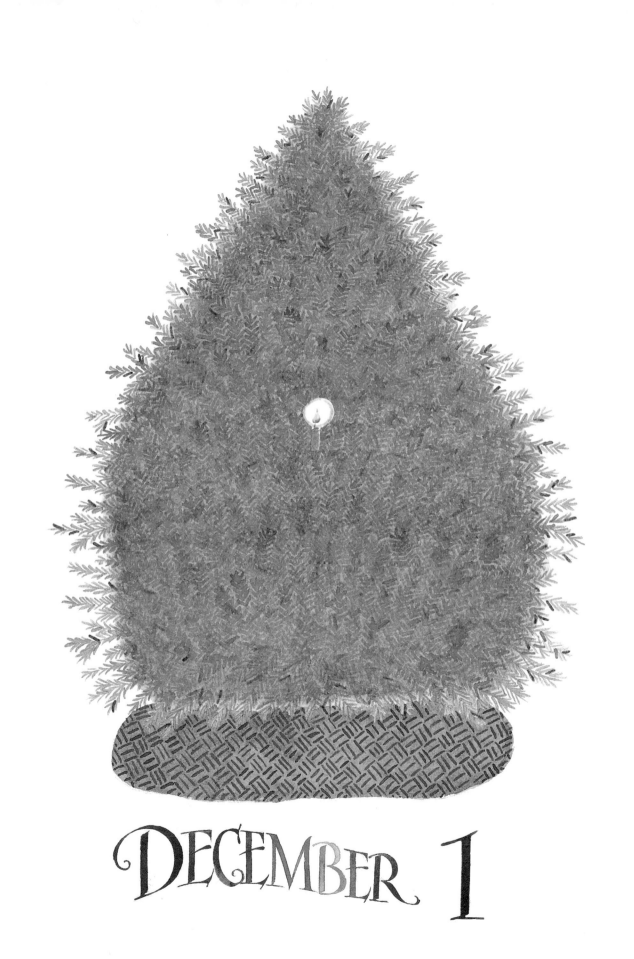

DECEMBER 1

When God first made people, the Bible says that He made them "in His image"! That doesn't mean that if we could see Adam and Eve we would know exactly what God looks like. But it *does* mean that He made us to be like Him; He made us holy.

A lot of people think that being holy means you have to be perfect and never make a mistake. But holy actually comes from the same word as whole. To be holy means that God made us complete.

When Adam and Eve disobeyed God, they were no longer complete because their hearts had become broken by sin. God, who is complete could no longer have companionship with them because their sin had made them incomplete. But God had a plan! He planned to send His Son, Jesus, to earth so that He could take our sin upon Himself and we could once again be able to live in companionship with God.

This month, as you read through this book, we're going to be learning about God's great love gift to us—Jesus. First we'll be talking about the events that happened around Jesus' birth. We want to have a clear picture of all the things that happened leading to Jesus' birth, and how God brought about the miracle of our salvation.

Then, we're going to be talking about how our celebration shows us a picture of Jesus. Did you know that many of the things we do to celebrate at Christmas teach us things about the Lord?

Lastly, we'll be learning about some of Jesus' names and titles. The Bible lists many different names for Jesus—kind of like nicknames. Learning about these names helps us understand why Jesus had to come and why we needed saving.

As you learn about the beliefs behind our celebration, remember that Christmas began in heaven! God loved us *first*!

Before we ever knew Him, before we ever heard of Him, actually, even before we were ever born—He loved us and had a plan to bring us into fellowship with Him. The Bible says, "Here is matchless love, not that we chose to love God, but that He chose to love us and sent His Son to save us" (1 John 4:10).

Joy to the World

Isaac Watts

ANTIOCH
Attr. to George F. Handel
Arr. by Lowell Mason

If you're planning to have an Advent calendar with your children, this is the day to begin!

Advent calendars are an exciting way for children to actually *see* the countdown to Christmas. It builds anticipation, and as they get a little older and understand how a calendar works, it can even help cut down on the number of times you're asked, "How many more days *until* Christmas?"

There are lots of ways to have an Advent calendar. You can make them or buy them, and almost anything can *become* an Advent calendar! You can purchase 24 small gifts per child, wrap them, place them in a basket, then allow the child to open one per day until Christmas. If this is impractical financially, fill a jar with 24 notes per child. Write special privileges or activities on each note, such as, "Let's bake cookies today," or "You can stay up 30 minutes past your bedtime tonight." For small children, a fun idea might be to have a small manger. (You can make a "manger" out of a shoe box covered with wood-look paper.) Let the child put in a handful of hay or straw each day. He can "make a bed for baby Jesus." Then on Christmas Day, let him put a doll wrapped in "swaddling clothes" in the manger. (If you have a daughter, she might like to "donate" a doll to be baby Jesus; if you have only sons, an inexpensive doll would be a nice addition to your Christmas decorations.) A jar filled with Christmas candies with a "one per day" rule can also be an Advent calendar. You could even set aside 24 ornaments and let each child add an ornament to the tree each day so that it becomes more and more decorated as you approach THE DAY.

Use one of these ideas, or one of your own and make *this* Advent a time of joyful anticipation for your family.

CHRISTMAS COUNTDOWN

· · · · · · · · · · · · · ·

Are you going out of town sometime
during the holidays? Hotel and airline
reservations should have been finalized
by Thanksgiving weekend. If you have
not yet completed your arrangements,
finish them today.

"*Every good gift and
every perfect gift is
from above,
and comes down from
the Father of lights.*"

James 1:17

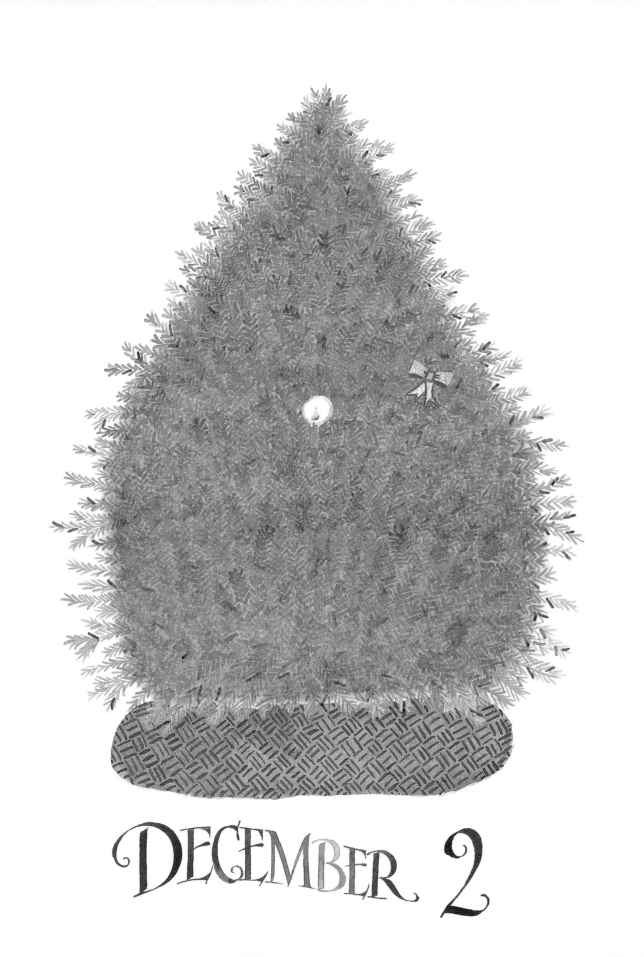

DECEMBER 2

The story of Jesus' birth has everything a really exciting story needs! It has a brave hero and heroine, long journeys, visits from heavenly beings, a bad guy, and a prince who grows up to be the King.

The story begins thousands of years ago in a far away village called Nazareth. One day, the Angel Gabriel visited a girl named Mary and told her that she would have a son who would grow up to save everyone from their sin. Gabriel also went to Joseph, Mary's fiance, and explained to him that this child was a gift from God . . . the son that Mary would have was actually the Son of God! Mary and Joseph both said yes to God's plan for their lives, and that makes them very, very brave.

Soon, they had to make the long journey to Bethlehem to pay their taxes to the Roman government. These days, we only have to mail our taxes from wherever we live. And if we have to go anywhere, we can just hop in our car and go. But Mary probably rode on a donkey, and Joseph probably walked. They went on a long, dusty road in a large crowd of noisy, jostling people who were also on the way to pay their taxes.

They finally arrived in Bethlehem, but the city was so crowded that there was no place for them to stay except in a barn, where Mary gave birth to her son, Jesus. Even though He was born in a barn, angels sang; and even though His family was very poor, wise men followed a star to visit Him.

But then, wicked King Herod heard about the birth of this child. He knew that the wise men had gone to visit Him and that they believed He would one day be King. Herod didn't like that. He didn't want anybody to be king except him, so he decided that he would find the Baby Jesus and kill Him.

That night, an angel came and warned Joseph. He told Joseph to take Mary and the baby and travel to another country called Egypt, where Herod would not be able to find them. Eventually Herod died, and Joseph took his family back to Nazareth, where Jesus grew up.

When Jesus was grown, He healed many people, and preached to them about how much God loves them and wants them to love Him too. But again, wicked people heard about Jesus. They saw the crowds of people who followed Him and believed in Him. They wanted all the people to follow them and do what they said, so they decided to kill Jesus . . . and this time they succeeded.

But this too was part of God's plan because Jesus died on the cross for our sins, and when He rose from the dead, He became the King of heaven. He promised that anyone who chooses to follow Him can receive great joy here on earth, and life forever with Him in heaven.

The First Noel

English Carol, before 1823

Traditional Melody
From Sandys' "Christmas Carols" 1833

1. The first No - el the an - gel did say, Was to cer - tain poor
2. They look - ed up and saw a star Shin - ing in the
3. And by the light of that same star Three Wise Men
4. Then let us all with one ac - cord Sing prais - es

shep - herds in fields as they lay; In fields where they lay keep - ing their
east, be - yond them far, And to the earth it gave great
came from coun - try far; To seek for a king was their in -
to our heav - en - ly Lord Who hath made heaven and earth of

Refrain

sheep, On a cold win - ter's night that was so deep.
light, And so it con - tin - ued both day and night. No - el, No -
tent, And to fol - low the star wher - ev - er it went.
naught, And with His blood man - kind hath bought.

el, No - el, No - el,__ Born is the King of Is - ra - el.

21

When my husband and I first got married we could hardly wait to go over to our parents' homes so that Christmas could "start." We had no decorations, no traditions, and, on college students' salaries, no food!

But we soon realized that we were faced with the pleasant task of planning how Christmas would be at our house and starting our own traditions. So we borrowed a few from our parents, added some of our own, combined things from our two families, and came up with a "Bauer kind of Christmas!"

What's nice is that we can add to or change our family traditions any time. There are no rules! As our children grow and their interests change, we can add or subtract whatever we want so that Christmas is constantly new and exciting but has the anchor of tradition woven throughout. Be prepared for the kids to offer their opinions, though! After my brothers and sister and I were all married, my dad asked if we ever had the traditional Christmas morning breakfast that we had grown up with. The answer was four very quick no's. To my parents' amazement, they found out that none of the four of us had ever liked it!

Starting a tradition can be as simple or elaborate as you want. One family I know has a tradition of always putting new toothbrushes in everyone's stockings. Another family tries to go to Disneyland each Christmastime to admire the Magic Kingdom decorations. One thing my husband and I have done is to save a Christmas stamp from each year since we've been married. The designs are always Christmas-themed, and it's a rather whimsical history of how things have changed since our marriage. We have them in a frame and add a new one each year.

Maybe your family would enjoy doing something like including a visit to a convalescent home or an elderly person in your church. Churches usually have extra events during Christmas. See if your whole family could help out in the child care program one evening. Include your neighbors at Christmas. Take them cookies or coffee cake. Or if you're really ambitious, have a neighborhood holiday open house.

Another good "tradition brainstorming source" is the library. Look up traditions from other countries. Browse through cookbooks and try some new Christmas goodies. Or borrow several craft books and make a few of your gifts this year.

And don't be afraid to borrow ideas from friends! If imitation is really the sincerest form of flattery, I'm sure they would be thrilled to share their ideas with you!

CHRISTMAS COUNTDOWN

· · · · · · · · · · · · · · ·

If you're planning to do any mail-order shopping, all orders should be placed this week. Ask for an order number and make sure you understand their return policy. Keep a record of your orders and the companies' telephone numbers in case there is a problem with anything. One friend gloated each year that all of his Christmas shopping was done by the end of November—all via catalog and from the comfort of his own armchair! It's definitely worth considering.

Also, make sure that any airmail packages and cards to Europe and the Far East are sent out today.

*"When Jesus ascended
into heaven,
He took prisoner
everything that holds
us prisoner.
And on top of that,
He gave us gifts!"*

Ephesians 4:8

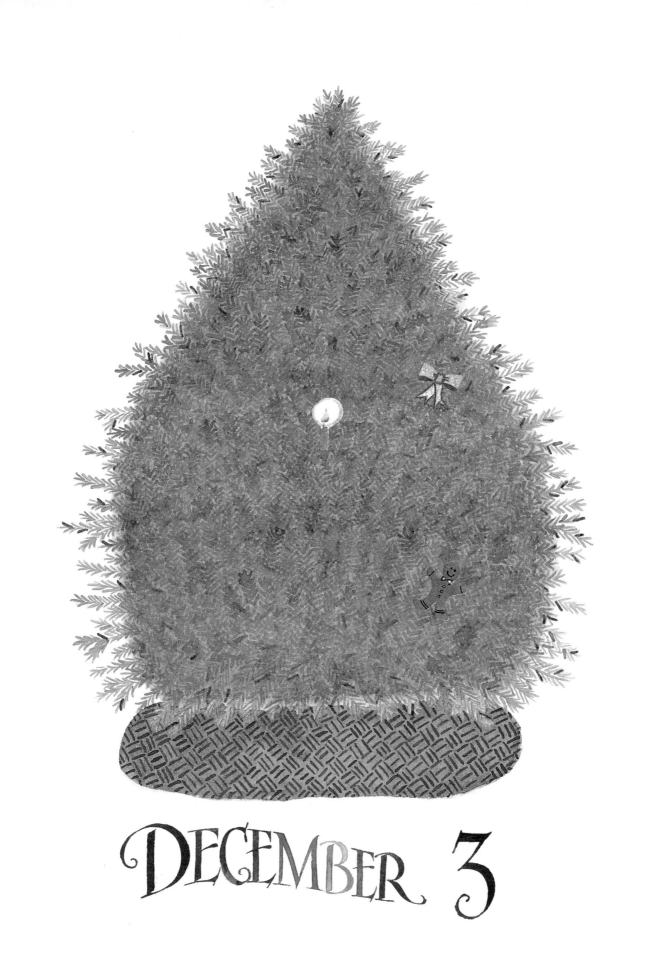

DECEMBER 3

God's Word is full of examples of God keeping His promises to people. The Bible calls them "prophecies," and they are promises that God not only makes, but that He Himself keeps.

He promised Abraham that he would have a son, although it looked pretty unlikely to Abraham. But he did have a son and it was when he was 100 years old! (And you thought your Mom and Dad were old!) Joseph was given promises by God. He saw that there was something great that God wanted to do with his life. Joseph's brothers laughed at him; but God kept His promise anyway. David knew he was to be king of Israel. The Prophet Samuel had spoken a word from God! That wasn't very much comfort when David was hiding in the wilderness from King Saul who wanted to kill him. But guess what: God kept His promise and David did become king.

God also gave many promises about the coming of the Messiah—the Promised One who would bring salvation to all people. Hundreds of years before Jesus' birth, God told where He would be born: "Bethlehem . . . out of you shall come forth the One to be ruler in Israel" (Micah 5:2). God promised that Jesus' coming would free us from our sin: "All we like sheep have gone astray; we have turned, everyone, to his own way; and the Lord has laid on Him the iniquity of us all" (Isa. 53:6).

After Jesus was born, God kept giving promises. There were promises given to Joseph and Mary: that Jesus would bring a light to the Gentiles (Luke 2:32). He made promises to the first Christians that they would minister in Jesus' name and He would bless them (Mark 16:15-18). Paul's life was spared through God's promises (Acts 27:24-25). And the Bible even ends with the promise of Jesus' return (Rev. 22:20-21).

That's a lot of promises! But do you know what's just as exciting? The Lord wants to give you promises about your life! Sometimes they will be things to share with someone else to pray over, and sometimes they will be things to think about in your own heart. Either way, they will be things to give to the Lord and let Him fulfill . . . because He always keeps His promises.

Maybe God will put a big dream in your heart that people will laugh at, like with Joseph. Maybe it will be something that seems impossible, like with David. But 1 Kings 8:56 says, "Not a single word has ever failed of all God's good promises." And just like God kept His promises to all of those people, He will keep His promises to you too.

O Come, O Come Emmanuel

Latin Hymn
Trans. by John M. Neale

VENI EMMANUEL
Thomas Helmore

1. O come, O come, Em - man - u - el, And ran - som cap - tive
2. O come, Thou Rod of Jes - se, free Thine own from Sa - tan's
3. O come, Thou Day-spring, come and cheer Our spir - its by Thine
4. O come, Thou Key of Da - vid, come, And o - pen wide our

Is - ra - el, That mourns in lone - ly ex - ile here.
tyr - an - ny; From depths of hell Thy peo - ple save,
ad - vent here; And drive a - way the shades of night,
heaven - ly home; Make safe the way that leads on high,

Un - til the Son of God ap - pear. Re - joice! Re - joice! Em -
And give them vic - tory o'er the grave. Re - joice! Re - joice! Em -
And pierce the clouds and bring us light! Re - joice! Re - joice! Em -
And close the path to mis - er - ry. Re - joice! Re - joice! Em -

man - u - el Shall come to thee, O Is - ra - el!
man - u - el Shall come to thee, O Is - ra - el!
man - u - el Shall come to thee, O Is - ra - el!
man - u - el Shall come to thee, O is - ra - el!

"Advent" means "coming," and an Advent wreath is a great way to keep our focus where it belongs: on Jesus' coming.

The Advent wreath originated in Europe and was a part of the religious celebration. Each of the four candles represents a different aspect of the events leading to Jesus' birth. Traditionally, they are the Prophecy Candle, representing hope; the Bethlehem Candle, representing faith; the Angel's Candle, representing peace; and the Shepherd's Candle, representing joy. The center candle is Christ's Candle and represents love.

The Advent wreath consists of a wreath or greenery twined candelabra fitted with four candles. One candle is lit each Sunday leading to Christmas. Then on Christmas Day, a fifth candle—usually larger than the other four—is placed in the center of the wreath celebrating the birth of the Light of the world.

The celebration of the Advent wreath also includes reading Scriptures showing both the Old Testament prophecies regarding the coming of the Messiah and the New Testament fulfillment of those promises.

Because Sundays fall on different dates each year, we've placed the devotionals that go with each candle, throughout the book for you to use as your celebration determines. Listed below are the devotionals, along with a Scripture reading to go with each candle.

The Prophecy Candle
Devotional is on December 3
Scripture reading: Isaiah 7:14, 9:6-7; Luke 1:30-35

The Bethlehem Candle
Devotional is on December 10
Scripture reading: Micah 5:2; Luke 2:1-7

The Angel's Candle
Devotional is on December 17
Scripture reading: Isaiah 52:7; Luke 2:8-14; 4:18-19

The Shepherd's Candle
Devotional is on December 22
Scripture reading: Ezekiel 34:23; Luke 2:15-20; John 10:11

Christ's Candle
Devotional is on December 24
Scripture reading: Isaiah 9:2; Luke 2:30-32

CHRISTMAS COUNTDOWN

• • • • • • • • • • • •

Make a Christmas Master Calendar today. A little organization now will pay off all month long! Make sure you include everyone's activities. Are there any school or office gatherings? How about that soccer end-of-season party? Do you need to schedule any haircut or doctor's appointments? Does your daughter still have her piano lessons this month or are they taking some time off? Get everything on your calendar. Other things to include: Are there any holiday meals or parties that will be at your house? Church activities? School Christmas program? Set aside decorating days now. Will you be having any out-of-town guests? Put their flight information on the arrival date of your calendar.

And while you're working on your calendar, make a few phone calls and arrange for any baby-sitting you may need. This may also be a great time to schedule a "baby-sitting swap" with a friend . . . and when you arrange it, be sure to put it on your calendar!

"*The gifts and purpose
of God can
never be canceled.
They are forever.*"

Romans 11:29

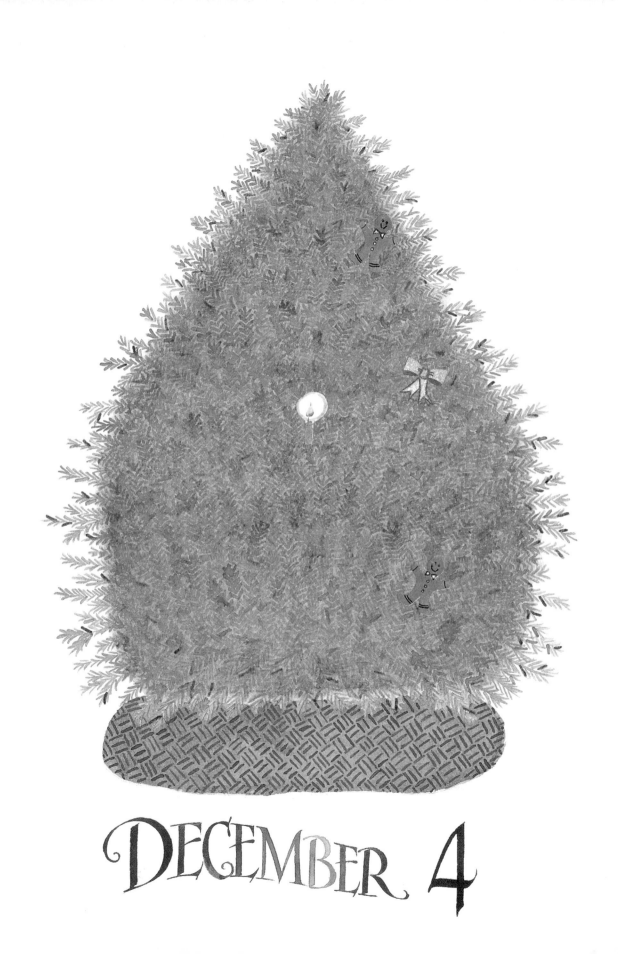

DECEMBER 4

Mary must have been a pretty amazing person!

First of all, an angel comes and gives her a message from God. (I want to hear messages from God, but I think an angel would scare me to death!) Then, she agrees to do exactly what God has told her to do. (I'm willing to do that, but it's really hard sometimes.) Lastly, not only did she *say* she would obey, she *did* obey. . . . And because she obeyed, God brought a blessing to the whole world! Just think—the Christmas story all began with Mary saying yes to God.

I think that makes her a pretty amazing person. But God wants all of us to be amazing people. Amazing people are people who obey the Lord, and from Mary we can learn about three things she did that will make you the amazing person God wants you to be! Mary had *listening ears*, an *obedient heart*, and *willing hands*. She lived in such a way that when God spoke to her, she could hear Him. She had a heart that wanted to obey, and her actions went along with what her heart wanted—she actually did what she said.

Now God doesn't just let the years when we're kids go by and then when we're grown up, say, "OK—now that you're all grown up, you can figure out how you're going to listen and obey Me all by yourself." Instead, He gives us a whole growing up time to practice! We start learning to hear and obey God by hearing and obeying our parents. Learning to obey is a very important thing, and Mom and Dad teach obedience so that when you are older and God talks to you, you will already have learned how to obey, and you can obey Him. Right now, then, while you're young, you need to be learning to live with listening ears so that you can hear when Mom and Dad call you, or give you instructions. Then you need to respond with an obedient heart and willing hands that are ready to obey your parents . . . and Jesus.

The best part, though, is that someday God will talk to you, and tell you what He wants you to do with your life, just like He did with Mary. Maybe it won't be with an angel, but He will talk to you. And when He does . . . obey Him. Because when we obey the Lord, He brings a blessing to us and to all those around us—just like He did with Mary!

Let's ask Him to help us right now. "Dear Jesus, Give me ears to hear Mom and Dad. Help me to obey with my heart and my hands. And someday when You speak to me about what You want me to do with my life, help me to hear and obey You too. Amen."

Take My Life and Let It Be

Frances R. Havergal   Henri A. César Malan

1. Take my life and let it be Con-se-crat-ed,
2. Take my feet and let them be Swift and beau-ti-
3. Take my lips and let them be Filled with mes-sa-
4. Take my love, my God, I pour At Thy feet its

Lord, to Thee; Take my hands and let them move —
ful for Thee; Take my voice and let me sing —
ges for Thee; Take my sil-ver and my gold, —
treas-ure store; Take my-self and I will be —

At the im-pulse of Thy love,— At the im-pulse of Thy love.
Al-ways, on-ly, for my King,— Al-ways, on-ly, for my King.
Not a mite would I with-hold,— Not a mite would I with-hold.
Ev-er, on-ly, all for Thee,— Ev-er, on-ly all for Thee.

Cooking can be a major project in December . . . not just for parties, either! Just getting three square meals on the table each day can be a real challenge. So here are a few suggestions to help mealtimes be eventful in an already-too-eventful month!

First, encourage your children to help with meal preparation. You're going to have to prepare meals anyway, so why not spend the time together! For the preschool set, one friend suggested, "Let them 'help' by sitting them on the kitchen floor and giving them some measuring cups and a bowl of dried beans. They'll think they're helping and you won't hear from them for a *long* time!" The bigger children can set the table, wash and chop vegetables, help with mixing and stirring. (My kids' all-time favorite thing to do is unwrap bouillon cubes and throw them into soup!) Let the kids also help out with meal planning. They may even have some good ideas that are simple enough for them to prepare without you.

You might consider using lots of paper plates for family meals. It will cut way down on your kitchen clean-up time. One year I bought the children a package of Christmas paper plates from the stationers. They used them each day for breakfast and thought it was great fun to have Santa smiling up at them each morning!

During December, I usually try to keep meals simple, but fun. Breakfast and lunch don't generally change much, even during holiday times, but old-fashioned standbys like pancakes for breakfast, and soup and sandwiches for lunch are nourishing and leave everybody ready to face another day at top speed.

One of my favorite easy dinners is roast chicken . . . it's fast, it's simple, and if you throw some cut-up potatoes and carrots in to bake with it, it's a fairly complete meal. Best of all, it makes the house smell wonderful! This is also a good time of year to break out the Crockpot for soups and stews; and the microwave is always handy for reheating anything. On evenings that you aren't rushed, make a double batch of a favorite casserole and freeze half for one of those extra-busy days. One night, make a beef stew and stuff it into a pumpkin to bake. It looks festive and the pumpkin can be scooped out to be the squash in the stew! Occasionally, we'll also have a "baked potato bar" for dinner where everyone makes their own potatoes. I bake 2 or 3 potatoes per person (5 or 6 for my teenagers!) and then provide all the toppings: cheese, onions, bacon bits, chili, broccoli, plain yogurt, salsa . . . whatever you like! It's quick, healthy, and easy.

And when you're really swamped, call out for pizza!

CHRISTMAS COUNTDOWN

● ● ● ● ● ● ● ● ● ●

Christmastime is here, and there are lists galore! Just think how easy Santa Claus has it—he only has to figure out a naughty and nice list. But a mother's lists seem to go on forever! Here are a few lists you may want to prepare:

GIFT LIST: List everyone; this is not the time to trust your memory! Also include any hostess gifts, office party gifts, and materials needed for homemade gifts. Are there gifts you have purchased throughout the year? Do you have ideas of what you want to buy for each person? Write those on your list too along with sizes where needed.

BAKING LIST: Are you planning to bake fruitcake this year? Did you promise to bring cupcakes for one of the children's class parties? Are you and a group of friends involved in a "cookie swap"? Put it all on your baking list! Get your recipes together and clip them to your list, along with a baking grocery list.

CHRISTMAS CARD LIST: Do you want to make any additions to or deletions from last year's Christmas card list? Are there any addresses you need to update? This is the time to do it!

MISCELLANEOUS LIST: Make a list of all the miscellaneous things you need to purchase. Do you need Christmas cards? How about wrapping paper, tissue paper, ribbon, and tape? Don't forget postage, batteries, and film. And while you're at it, pick up some thank-you notes.

PARTY MENUS: Plan your menus ahead of time and make out your grocery list now so that you can take advantage of sale prices throughout the month. Call people to make any food assignments now and mark them on your calendar. Don't worry about reminding them later; if they forget, they'll call you!

"*We should receive
the gift of giving and
the fellowship of
serving one another.*"

2 Corinthians 8:4

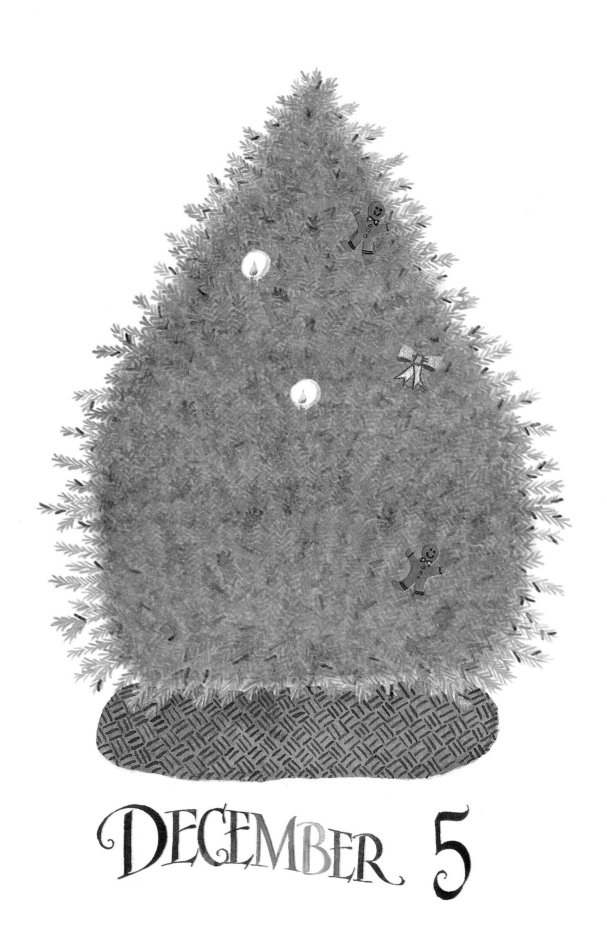

DECEMBER 5

Every day is a busy day when you're a kid! You might run around with the dog, help in the garden, read a great book, or do homework. Maybe you'll skate, ride bikes, do chores, watch TV, and set the table. But no matter what you do, you're still listening. Even when there is all kinds of noise going on, if Mom or Dad calls, you'll hear. You know why? Because you listen for the people you love. Even when there are a lot of other things going on, not only are your ears listening, but your heart is listening too.

When Jesus would preach, He would sometimes end His sermons by saying, "He who has ears to hear, let him hear," and I think that's what He meant. He wanted people to be listening to the things He said—not just with their ears but with their hearts too. And that's true today . . . Jesus wants us to be listening for His voice.

He talks to people in many different ways. Sometimes He talks to us through His Word—the Bible. That's why you should be reading your Bible every day. When you read your Bible, the Lord can show you verses that tell you how to behave or how to solve problems. God also talks to us in our hearts and lets us know exactly what we're supposed to do in different situations. The Bible lists other ways that God talks to people. He talked to Joseph in dreams. The Bible says that He talked to Moses "face-to-face, as a man speaks to his friend." Samuel heard actual words, and David received beautiful songs from the Lord. Paul saw visions, and Elijah heard God's "still, small voice."

I don't know how the Lord will choose to talk to you, but He will always be with you and help you. You never need to feel lonely (even if you're the new kid); and you never need to feel afraid (even if it's thundering outside!). He will help you to make right choices about the things you do. He will remind you of the things you've studied when it's time to take a test. He will encourage you to do your very best at all times. And He will always tell you how much He loves you.

All it takes to hear His voice are ears to hear Him and a heart to love Him. God wants to talk to you—just as simply as Mom or Dad does. Love Him. Listen for Him. He's waiting to talk to you.

Angels We Have Heard On High

Source Unknown
Old French Carol

1. An-gels we have heard on high, Sweet-ly sing-ing o'er the plains
2. Shepherds, why this ju-bi-lee? Why your joy-ous strains pro-long?
3. Come to Beth-le-hem, and see Him whose birth the an-gels sing;
4. See with-in a man-ger laid Je-sus, Lord of heav'n and earth!

And the moun-tains in re-ply Ech-o back their joy-ous strains.
Say what may the ti-dings be, Which in-spire your heav'n-ly song?
Come, a-dore on bend-ed knee Christ the Lord, the new-born King.
Ma-ry, Jo-seph, lend your aid, With us sing our Sav-iour's birth.

Refrain

Glo - - - ri-a in ex-cel-sis De - o, Glo - - - ri-a in ex-cel-sis De - o.

39

"Running errands" and "little children" seem to be mutually exclusive terms! But if you plan the day to include a few fun things for the kids and a lunch/rest time, things can go pretty smoothly.

If you're a stay-at-home Mom, try to go early to avoid as many crowds as possible. If you work, the dinner hour is a less crowded time at the local mall! Then plan "chore" errands and "fun" errands. Take a list of exactly where you will be going and what you will be doing or purchasing at each stop, and put them in order ahead of time so that you don't have to retrace your steps. Also, take along some non-messy snacks, such as raisins or nuts. If you don't want the hassle of having to stop for a meal, pack a fun "picnic" with Christmasy foods like peanut butter sandwiches on raisin bread, popcorn or trail mix, and candy canes for dessert. (And don't forget the diaper wipes for messy hands!)

Here are some errands to consider:

1. I go to the grocery store first because it's my favorite "one stop shop." Besides shopping for all of my baking supplies, I can buy wrapping paper, ribbon, cards, stocking stuffers, and even postage stamps!   By stopping at the market first, I can sometimes eliminate several other stops.

2. Stop at the post office and buy all the stamps you'll need for your Christmas cards (and thank-you notes too).

3. Buy all of your Christmas cards, wrapping paper, and ribbon. Let the kids help you pick these. You'll be surprised at what good taste they have! They would probably also enjoy picking out some special cards to send to Grandma and Grandpa. (Grandma and Grandpa will like it too!)

4. Do all of the Christmas shopping for Dad. Just wrap the gifts as soon as you get home to protect them from prying eyes; and, make *sure* the kids understand *exactly* what "keeping a secret" means! *shhhh!*

5. Pay a visit to Santa Claus.

6. Stop at the toy store. The kids will like it and you can get some good shopping ideas for them. Let them help choose gifts for any children on your list.

7. Do any "miscellaneous shopping." Find several small gifts to have available for office parties. Don't forget the boss. Purchase stocking stuffers.

CHRISTMAS COUNTDOWN

• • • • • • • • • • • • •

Send out your party invitations early in
the month to allow your guests plenty of
time to plan their calendars!

"*Every person should
enjoy what is produced
from his hard work.
It is the gift of God.*"

Ecclesiastes 3:13

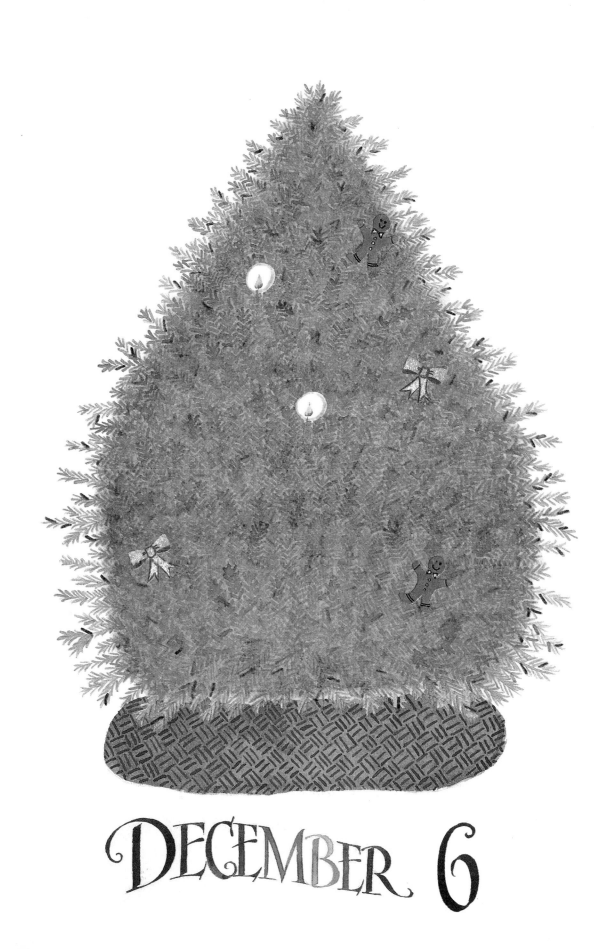

DECEMBER 6

Did you know that the Bible tells us the words to the very first Christmas carol? Right after the angel announced to Mary that she would give birth to Jesus, she sang a song!* ♪

It shouldn't surprise us that Mary would *sing* her praise to God at such a time. The Book of Job says that God created the whole world while the angels sang praises. The Psalms tell us over and over to sing praises to the Lord. It also tells us that praise makes us beautiful! Nehemiah says that praise makes us strong! And Isaiah says to sing to the Lord when He has done excellent things—which is all the time! So after the angel had come to Mary, she sang a song of praise and rejoicing. Her song also tells us the reasons why she was rejoicing:

First she said that she was praising the Lord because "Though I am not important, God has looked upon me." Mary knew that she couldn't do anything unless she had the Lord. She praised Him because even though she was helpless, God saw her and cared about her. Thank You, Lord, that You always take care of us! Mary recognized that without God's help she was nobody special. But look what she says next!

"From now on, everyone will say that I'm blessed!" Why? Because even though she knew she was no one special, God *made* her into someone special! And just like God had a plan for Mary's life, He has a great plan for each of our lives that no one else can do. That special plan will not only bless us, but will bless people around us! Thank You, Lord, that You have a plan for my life and You make me into someone really special.

Next Mary praises the Lord because, "He who is mighty has done great things for me!" She thanks Him because "He is merciful and compassionate"—He understands everything we face; "He has exalted" us—and made us into someone special who can bless others; "He has fed" us—He *always* provides for *all* of our needs; "He is strong and helps" us; and "He speaks to" us.

When we hear Christmas carols ♪ this Christmas, let's remember the praise that was in Mary's heart when she sang that very first Christmas carol. There are a lot of good reasons to praise the Lord. . . . But the best one is the same one that Mary had . . . Jesus.

Let's sing our thanks to Him right now!

* Luke 1:46-55

Several years ago, my family fell into the habit of listening to secular radio. We weren't listening to "heavy metal"; *we* were listening to pretty love songs. But while I carry no brief against secular music, I did get a little tired of hearing my children going around the house singing, "I love you, baby."

One day I realized that if I surrounded my children with music that was spirit-strengthening, I would be living out the Lord's directive in Deuteronomy 6:6-7:

> And these words which I command you today shall be in your heart; you shall teach them diligently to your children, and shall talk of them when you sit in your house, when you walk by the way, when you lie down, and when you rise up.

Not only is music a great teacher, but it can bring comfort, help us memorize Scripture and apply character traits, bring understanding of spiritual principles, minister freedom to our lives (Ps. 32:6-7), dispel the works of the adversary (2 Chron. 20:20-21), and allow God's creative majesty full liberty to work in our homes and in our lives (Job 38:4-7). In our home, music has been applied in all of these ways.

A couple of years ago following an earthquake, my children sang, "God is my refuge and strength . . . though the earth be moved" (Ps. 46:1-2). The Word in song banished fear and brought comfort to them. We have watched the power of spiritual song break the grip of depression oppressing our home. We have seen God create new attitudes, new peace, new ideas, even new study habits as we've given ourselves to praise in prayer and in song.

And singing can be a lot of fun! From learning hymns in the car to twanging the theme to "The Beverly Hillbillies" around the dinner table, music has provided our family with a lot of entertainment!

Play music in the car and in the house! Learn some Christmas carols and go caroling. Sing a song together each night before bed. Sing a chorus of thanksgiving for your dinnertime prayer.

And having learned a lesson the hard way, there is now nothing more satisfying to me than to hear my children walking through the house singing, "You, Lord, are greater than my greatest joy."

Our children will live out what we put into them. Let's put in things that establish eternal truths in their hearts.

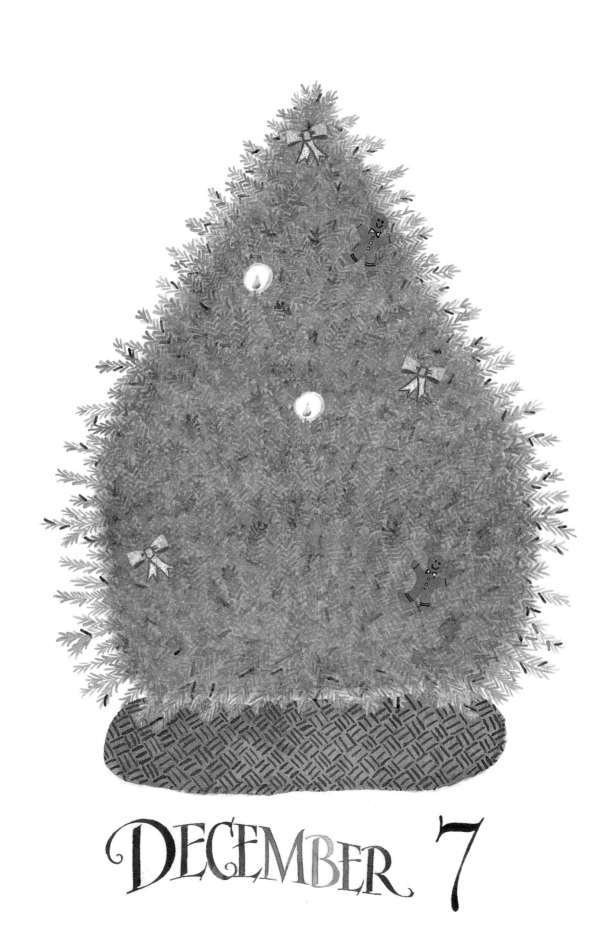

DECEMBER 7

Which do you think is more important: Christmas or Easter? They are *both* important holidays. And you get vacations from school for *both* of them. And they are *both* about Jesus. So how can you tell which is more important?

Well, Easter could never have happened if Jesus hadn't come at Christmas, because the reason He came at all was to save us. And without Jesus' sacrifice at Easter, His coming at Christmas would have had no meaning; it would just have been the birth of another baby. The two holidays are linked together! So the answer to "which holiday is more important" is *BOTH*!

And our Christmas tree tells the story of *both*! Of course, it reminds us that Jesus came as a baby, because it is the center of our decorations and gift-giving celebration. But it is also a picture of Jesus' cross. In fact, the Bible even calls the cross a tree! First Peter 2:24 says that Jesus "bore our sins in His own body on the tree." On the "tree," Jesus gave the ultimate sacrifice—His life—and when He did, His blood flowed down to the foot of the cross. In the same way, we lay our gifts to one another at the bottom of our Christmas trees, to remind us of the greatest gift we ever received: our salvation.

The Christmas tree not only reminds us of Jesus' cross, but also of His promise to give us "everlasting life." We use evergreen trees at Christmas because they stay green all year long and don't show signs of withering or dying. In that way, our Christmas tree can remind us that Jesus said, "He who believes in Me has everlasting life" (John 6:47).

Lastly, the Christmas tree is a picture to us of what God does in our lives when we accept Him! Psalms says that the person who follows God's ways "shall be like a tree planted by the rivers of water . . . whose leaf also shall not wither; and whatever he does shall prosper" (1:3). And Psalm 92:12 promises that "the righteous shall flourish like a . . . tree."

This Christmas, when you look at your Christmas tree, don't spend all of your time thinking only about the presents you will be opening in a few days. Spend some of your time remembering what the tree is a picture of and thanking the Lord for the gifts that He has given us: the gift of Jesus' coming at Christmas and the gift of our salvation at Easter.

Lord Jesus Christ

Jack W. Hayford

Traditional German Carol
Tannenbaum

Lord Je - sus Christ, Lord Je - sus Christ, to praise Your Name we ga - ther. Lord

Je - sus Christ, Lord Je - sus Christ, to praise Your Name we ga - ther. Be-

cause You came God's love is here. Be - cause You came God's love is here. Lord

Je - sus Christ, Lord Je - sus Christ, to praise Your Name we ga - ther.

We all wish that we could have a Christmas tree that would sparkle and shine like the ones in the florist shop display windows. But that usually is not the case with the hodge-podge of ornaments most of us have accumulated. Add to that the fact that most of us aren't interior decorators and that our "help" comes from little hands and, well . . . you get the picture! However, by following a few simple guidelines, our Christmas trees can be beautiful and the process full of fun from start to finish.

Decorating the Christmas tree, of course, starts with getting the tree. Before you make your purchase, stand where you want to place your tree and get a firm idea of the size of tree you will need (both in height and width). When you figure height, don't forget to add the height of your tree stand and your tree topper. Then whether you chop a tree, buy a tree, use an artificial tree, or plant a living tree, make the setting up of it a fun first step in the decorating process.

Once you actually start decorating, follow these rules:

1. The lights go on first. (Hint: Clear lights show off colorful ornaments better.)

2. Next, put your tree topper on.

3. Now put on the garland. (Hint: Always work from the top to the bottom whenever you put anything on the tree.)

4. If you have bows to put on your tree, they go on now! I like bows because you can fill in empty spaces with them. (Hint: If you don't use bows, try wrapping empty boxes to fill the empty spaces on your tree.)

5. The ornaments go on next. Put on all of one kind (or color) at one time for distribution purposes and to avoid color clumps. (Hint: Put the special or handmade ornaments on last. If you put them on first, they will be covered up with other decorations later.)

6. Remember to put smaller objects toward the top, and larger objects toward the bottom. Also, put heavier objects closer to the center of the tree.

7. Don't forget to water your tree regularly. (Hint: Avoid spills by letting the children water the tree with ice cubes.)

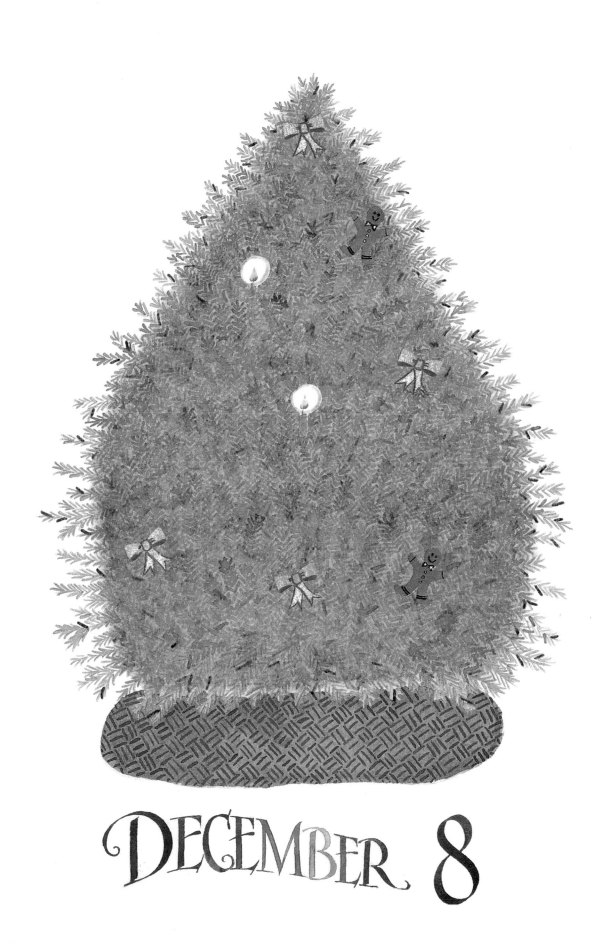

DECEMBER 8

When I was little, I liked to read stories about Jesus. He always seemed so kind and ready to help. I especially liked that He was brave enough to stand up to the "bad guys" because I knew I wasn't that brave. I also liked the fact that He loved *everyone*— especially children! I thought Jesus would be a great friend to have . . . and I wanted to be like Him. But I could only picture Him as a grown-up. If I was going to be like Him when I was a kid, I wanted to know what He was like when He was a kid!

We do know that He learned to be a carpenter from Joseph, so He must have had chores around the house and the workshop. I suppose He had to go to school. There is one verse, though, that describes Jesus as a child, and it gives us a pretty good idea of what He was like and how we can be like Him—even when we're still kids!

Luke 2:40 says, "And the Child [Jesus] grew and became strong in spirit, filled with wisdom; and the grace of God was upon Him." Later in that same chapter, we find out that Jesus had a solid grasp of Scripture even as a child. He was even teaching the teachers in the temple when He was 12! And it was Jesus' understanding of the Bible that brought that strength and wisdom and grace into His life . . . and it can do the same thing in yours!

Psalm 111:10 says, "The fear [or reverence] of the Lord is the beginning of wisdom; a good understanding have all those who do His commandments." Another verse says, "If you receive My words, and treasure My commands within you . . . then you will understand the fear of the Lord and find the knowledge of God" (Prov. 2:1-2, 5). And Psalm 119:28 asks the Lord to, "Strengthen [us] according to Your Word." Just think! The reason God gave us the Bible was to provide us with wisdom and strength!

Wisdom and strength are what goes into our hearts when we learn the Bible, but grace is what comes out! Ecclesiastes 10:12 tells us that "the words of a wise man's mouth are gracious." And in Colossians, Paul teaches us to "let your speech always be with grace" (4:6), and to "let the word of Christ dwell in you . . . singing with grace in your hearts to the Lord" (3:16).

So how can we become like Jesus? By being in the Word. We can read our Bibles. We can pay extra close attention when we go to Sunday School. We can carefully listen to the things that Mom and Dad teach us about the Lord. When we do that, the commandments that the Lord has given us in His Word will fill our hearts with wisdom and strength. Then the things we say and do will be full of the grace and kindness of the Lord, and every day we will become more and more like Him.

To Be Like Jesus

Traditional   Traditional

To be like Je-sus,   to be like Je-sus! My de-sire—   to be like Him!

All thru life's jour-ney   from earth to glo-ry, My de-sire—   to be like Him.

"Great peace have those who love Your law," promises Psalm 119:165. And if there is anything that I could ask for my children throughout their lives it would be peace—spiritual peace, emotional peace, physical peace, international peace; educational, economic, vocational, and domestic peace. "Peace" is truly the great cry of our time, the longing of every heart, and the "impossible dream" of each generation. Yet this Scripture gives a clear-cut course of action for attaining peace in every arena of life.

Deuteronomy 6:7 further exhorts parents, "You shall teach them [God's commands] diligently to your children, and shall talk of them when you sit in your house, when you walk by the way, when you lie down, and when you rise up." What an assignment! And the beginning is the biggest challenge.

We begin to instill in our children a love for God's Word by loving it ourselves—and living it. I'm not talking about a letter-of-the-law legalism, but a living, breathing, life-changing, principle-shaping Word of God that is applicable to every situation we face.

Begin by involving the Word in *your* life. Are you in the Word daily? Do you apply its promises and commands to your personal life? We can *tell* our children that the Bible is an important part of life, but we also have to *live* it. . . . Kids can spot a fake a mile away! Be in the Word every day. Draw on the spiritual nourishment that the Lord has provided. Let the Word of God in music fill your home and spirit with His peace and joy. As that happens in us, we can begin to impress a love for God's Word in the lives of our children.

When our children were small, we read a chapter in a Bible story book each day. We provided them with Bible music tapes as soon as they could talk well enough to sing along, and when they began to read, we gave them an easy-to-read Bible and encouraged them to read a portion of Scripture on their own each day. They have now accumulated pre-teen study Bibles, Bibles on tape, and even a comic strip Bible! We've memorized Scripture together, played Bible trivia games at dinner, and applied specific verses to problems each of the children have faced. Being in God's Word should be simple, interesting, and fun!

What would your children enjoy? What will "hook" them into digging for the treasure that has been given to us in God's Word? There's still time to slip another gift under the Christmas tree! Ask the Lord how you are to introduce His Word to your children and then watch as His peace begins to transform their lives into His image!

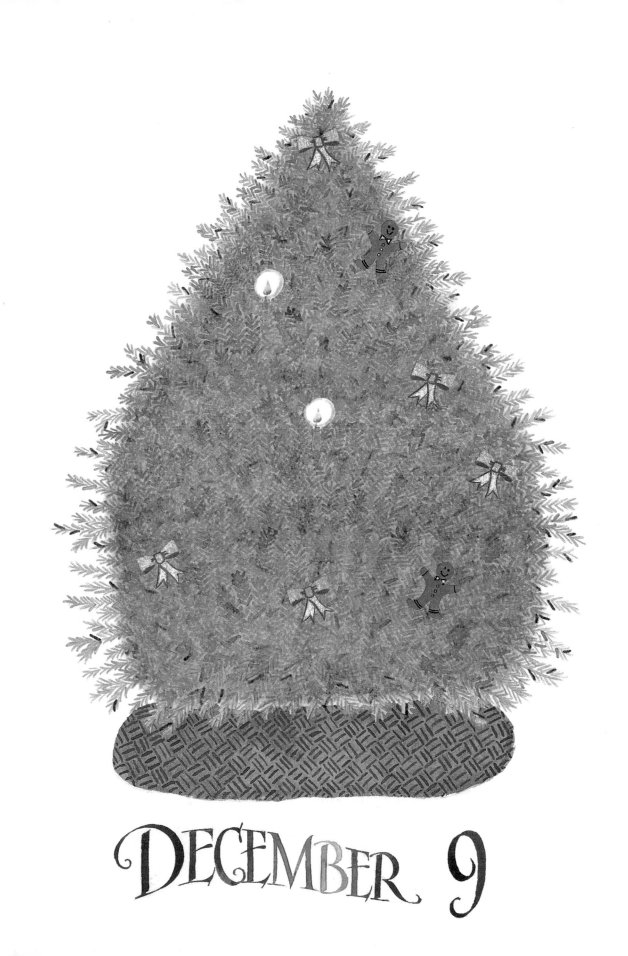

DECEMBER 9

One of my favorite things at Christmastime is to decorate the tree! But putting on the ornaments sometimes makes me think of fruit trees. You know— apple trees are covered with apples, orange trees are covered with oranges, and Christmas trees are covered with ornaments. I've wondered if maybe ornaments aren't "Christmas tree fruit"!

Each ornament is so beautiful, and many of them represent special things that have happened to us. Our family has ornaments from special vacations, ornaments from when each child was born, ornaments that were made at Sunday School. Maybe you have a lot of the same kinds of ornaments on your tree too. They are special ornaments because each one represents a gift—the gift of a person or the gift of a special memory.

The Bible says that every good gift comes from God (James 1:17). Let's name some of the gifts that God has put in our lives. Can you think of any gifts that are represented by the ornaments that you have on your Christmas tree? Say those too! And then, every time you look at your Christmas tree with its dozens of sparkling ornaments, thank the Lord that He's put so many good gifts into your life.

God doesn't want us to stop there, though; He has an even bigger plan! He wants to decorate US!

There are other gifts that the Bible says God gives us. They're called the "fruit of the Spirit." The fruit of the Spirit are love, joy, peace, patience, kindness, goodness, faithfulness, gentleness, self-control. Just like our Christmas trees are decorated with ornaments, God wants to decorate us with this wonderful fruit that makes us more like Him!

I think about God wanting to decorate me each time I decorate my Christmas tree. And I ask the Lord what new decorations He wants to put on me this year, because I want to have more every year! Would you like to have more decorations on you? Maybe you argue with your brother or sister and God wants to decorate you with self-control and peace. Or maybe you always want everything to happen *right now*! . . . and God wants to decorate you with patience. What are you going to ask Jesus to decorate you with this year?

Come, Thou Long Expected Jesus

Charles Wesley

HYFRYDOL
Rowland H. Prichard
Arr. by Ralph Vaughan Williams

1. Come, Thou long ex-pect-ed Je-sus, Born to set Thy peo-ple
2. Born Thy peo-ple to de-liv-er, Born a child and yet a

free; From our fears and sins re-lease us; Let us find our
king. Born to reign in us for-ev-er, Now Thy gra-cious

rest in Thee. Israel's strength and con-so-la-tion, Hope of
king-dom bring. By Thine own e-ter-nal Spir-it Rule in

all the earth Thou art; Dear De-sire of ev-ery
all our hearts a-lone; By Thine all suf-fi-cient

na-tion, Joy of ev-'ry long-ing heart.
mer-it, Raise us to Thy glo-rious throne. A-men.

Decorating the house is the Christmastime chore that has always seemed the most time consuming to me, but I've found that varying our decorating plan from year to year has made a bigger-than-life-sized job much easier to handle. One year, we decorated a room each day until we were all done. We also usually decorate the Christmas tree on a separate evening from working on the rest of the house. Once following a *very* trying year, we decided to put up only our tree. Then there have been the years that we've entered the "annual decorating marathon" and stayed up until two in the morning getting it all done at once! But one thing has always held true: we try to include our children as much as possible.

Children can put hooks on ornaments and hand them up the ladder. They can run errands and put up "unbreakable" ornaments. Older kids can cut greens, carry boxes in and out, vacuum up pine needles, and even decorate the tree! But when the kids are involved, there are a few rules to remember:

1. Keep the child's age and attention span in mind: big jobs for big kids, little jobs for little kids.

2. Let them work on a project that allows them to see a lot of progress. This isn't the time to ask them to sit and hold the glue gun for you! Let them hang up ornaments or arrange the nativity display.

3. Make sure you give them complete instructions. Take time to explain *everything*. What may be obvious to you, probably won't be obvious to them!

4. Allow them to have some decorations that are their own! Along with giving them ornaments each year that they hang on the Christmas tree, we let the children decorate their bedrooms. One year my kids made yards and yards of red and green paper chains and we strung them around the bedrooms. Include an unbreakable nativity set for each child to put in his or her room so that they can reenact the Christmas story again and again! One year I went into my sons' room where they had set up a wooden nativity set. Was I ever surprised when I saw that along with the Holy Family they had displayed a whole herd of stuffed animals, some army men, and a plastic dinosaur!

5. Plan for breaks. What may be another project to us is just more Christmas fun to our children. Don't be a slave-driver! Stop and admire everyone's work. Share some Christmas cookies. And relax, Mom! Enjoy what you've accomplished so far!

DECEMBER 10

ave you ever wondered how God makes His promises happen? I used to imagine God doing something kind of mysterious that made everything go the way He wanted it to. But as I grew up, I found that the way God usually makes His promises happen is through great planning! Mary and Joseph are a good example of how that happens.

God had promised Mary that her child was to be the Messiah. Mary would have known enough of the promises about Messiah's coming to know that He was supposed to be born in Bethlehem. That wasn't where Mary lived, and she could have spent all of her time worrying about how she could work it so that her baby could be born there. But she couldn't have made it happen on her own.

Instead, Caesar Augustus, the ruler of the Roman Empire, gave the reason for going there. God worked everything in such a way that Caesar suddenly decided that everyone should be taxed. In order to do that, they would have to go to the town of their birth. Joseph was born in Bethlehem, so to Bethlehem they went!

God planned the whole thing!

How to get to Bethlehem was Mary and Joseph's problem. But God used the things that were happening around them to get them where He wanted them to be when He wanted them to be there! And He did it so that He could cause a miracle to happen that would bring blessing to the whole world.

God wants to do the same kind of thing in each of our lives. We have talked before about God giving us promises. Sometimes when God gives people promises, they want to make the promise come true without His help. That never works. Whatever He promises, you will need His help for it to take place. You can't make it happen on your own.

That is what Bethlehem is a picture of: God bringing you to the place that He wants you to be so that He can do something great through you. God has different things for different people to do. And He tells people things at different times in their lives. No matter what God tells you or when He tells you, you can be sure that He will also bring about the perfect time for that to take place.

When God gives you promises, don't spend your time worrying about how they will happen. Listen to the Lord as He works in circumstances and talks to you through His Word. If you really want to do His will, He won't let you make a mistake. God will get you where you need to be when you need to be there so that He can work His great purpose in you.

Silent Night

Joseph Mohr

STILLE NACHT
Franz Gruber

1. Si - lent night! Ho - ly night! All is calm, all is bright 'Round yon
2. Si - lent night! Ho - ly night! Shep-herds quake at the sight! Glo - ries
3. Si - lent night! Ho - ly night! Son of God, love's pure light! Ra - diant

vir - gin moth-er and Child! Ho - ly In -fant, so ten-der and mild,
stream from heav-en a - far, Heav'n-ly hosts sing Al - le -lu - ia;
beams from Thy ho -ly face, With the dawn of re - deem -ing grace,

Sleep in heav - en - ly peace,— Sleep in heav - en - ly peace.—
Christ, the Sav -iour, is born,— Christ, the Sav -iour, is born. —
Je - sus, Lord, at Thy birth,— Je - sus, Lord, at Thy birth.—

I like to choose a theme and decorate our home a little differently each year. One year we used snowflakes; one year we made bows. Last year we put little gold foil fans all over the place. While we might make one purchase to add to our decorations, it's challenging and fun to come up with a theme that will use the decorations we already have in a new (and inexpensive) way.

One way to add to your family's decorations is to make them. Bread dough ornaments are always fun to make. Or give the children baskets of fruit and nuts to put around the house. Have them make paper snowflakes to cover with glitter and hang from the ceiling or in the windows. Let them hollow out apples to use as candle holders. Christmas stickers and coloring books add to their supply of ideas and keep them busy decorating packages and coloring pictures. One year we even had an art gallery and let the children hang up all of the holiday art that they had made at church, school, and home.

In addition to the family decorations, our children have their own decorations. Every year we give each of them a new Christmas tree ornament. These ornaments are often dated so that they commemorate the year. But they have also received ornaments as birthday gifts (for our December boy) and vacation mementos. The children have added small toys and projects that they've made at church or school too. We all get to enjoy these ornaments now, but eventually they will go with the children when they grow up and leave home! Best of all, these decorations will already have years of happy memories attached to them.

Scent as a decoration is fun too. Keep potpourri burning on the stove. Put a pot of water on and add any combination of cinnamon, nutmeg, and cloves. Adding some sliced oranges or a little bay leaf is a nice variation. Also try putting some cinnamon sugar in a disposable pie pan and baking in the oven for that "just baked" smell. Add a little ginger or nutmeg. Play with the spices and see what kind of combinations you come up with. Though neither my husband nor I drink coffee, one of my favorite smells is vanilla flavored coffee, so I'll occasionally bubble some of that on the stove just for the smell! I also try and buy several scents such as gingerbread, pine, or bayberry to spray all around the house.

Use your imagination and see what ideas you come up with to fill your home with decorations that delight every sense: see the tree, hear the music, smell the spices, feel the warmth, and taste the goodies!

CHRISTMAS COUNTDOWN

• • • • • • • • • • • • • •

Any packages you want to send by parcel post within the continental United States need to be sent today.

"God has put gifts in you.
So stir them up!
Don't be afraid to use them,
because God has
filled you with strength,
love, and wisdom. "

2 Timothy 1:6-7

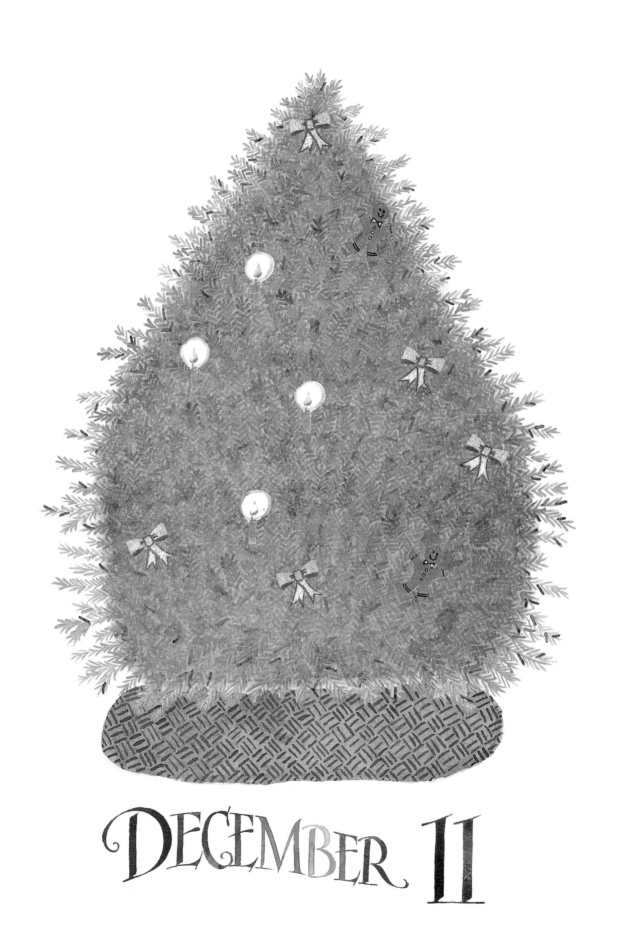

DECEMBER 11

When Mary and Joseph first arrived in Bethlehem, there was no place for them to stay. Everyone sent them away except for one innkeeper who felt sorry for them and offered them his barn. It has always amazed me that Jesus—the Son of God and the One who would be the King of kings —was born in a stable filled with dirty, stinky animals; and that His first bed was a trough filled with hay.

It also seems sad to think that anyone would ever have turned Him away. Could the innkeeper have given Mary and Joseph his room? Or could one of the villagers have seen that Mary was about to have her baby and helped her in some way? Instead, no one helped them and they wound up in a barn.

Today, Jesus is still looking for a place to stay, but now He isn't looking for houses to live in, He is looking for hearts. That is why He came . . . to live in us.

Jesus said, "I have come that you may have life, and that you may have it abundantly." That means that He doesn't just give us "regular life," He gives us extra special life! First, He comes in to live in our hearts. Then He fills us with so much of Himself that our lives become more than we could ever have thought! He fills us with more joy, and more love, and more hope, and more of Him! Everything that was in our lives before becomes better when we add Jesus!

He is looking for hearts to let Him in so that He can do new things in us every day. In a way, it's the same as what happened with Mary in that barn . . . she had something new happen with her, and the Lord wants something new to happen with each of us too.

Your new thing probably won't be a baby. But, then again, maybe it will be! Maybe there's going to be a new baby in your family. Jesus will fill your heart with so much love that you'll love *everybody* more—Mom and Dad AND the new baby!

Is there a new kid at school who is afraid or lonely? Maybe Jesus wants you to be a friend to them. Maybe He wants you to pay more attention to your lessons at school so that you can become a better student—someone who is honoring the Lord in everything you do! Maybe you need to work on truthfulness, or sharing, or diligence. Whatever it is, Jesus will help that new thing happen in you!

O Little Town of Bethlehem

Phillips Brooks   Lewis H. Redner

1. O lit-tle town of Beth-le-hem, How still we see thee lie!
2. For Christ is born of Ma-ry; And gath-ered all a-bove,
3. How si-lent-ly, how si-lent-ly The won-drous Gift is giv'n!
4. O ho-ly Child of Beth-le-hem, De-scend to us, we pray;

A-bove thy deep and dream-less sleep The si-lent stars go by;
While mor-tals sleep, the an-gels keep Their watch of won-d'ring love.
So God im-parts to hu-man hearts The bless-ings of His Heav'n.
Cast out our sin and en-ter in, Be born in us to-day.

Yet in thy dark streets shin-eth The ev-er-last-ing Light;
O morn-ing stars, to-geth-er Pro-claim the ho-ly birth,
No ear may hear His com-ing; But in this world of sin,
We hear the Christ-mas an-gels The great glad ti-dings tell,

The hopes and fears of all the years Are met in thee to-night.
And prais-es sing to God the King, And peace to men on earth.
Where meek souls will re-ceive Him still, The dear Christ en-ters in.
O come to us, a-bide with us, Our Lord Em-man-u-el.

67

In all of the decorating, don't forget the outside of your house! If you're fortunate enough to have snow for Christmas, you're halfway there! Your house already looks like a Christmas card! Build a family of snowmen on the front lawn. Or light your house in a way that will show off an icicle fringe or a snow-frosted fence.

Lights outside are a *must* at Christmas! And there are as many different kinds of lights and ways to put them on as there are people! There are different colors and sizes of Christmas lights. There are lights that go off and on in color patterns, or lights that twinkle like the stars. String Japanese lanterns across your yard, or outline your walkways with luminarias. My personal favorite look is large-sized colored lights on the house, and small-sized white lights on the shrubs. It's a look that I have never gotten tired of and enjoy so much that I finally asked my husband to put permanent hooks all along the roof line to make hanging the lights each year an easier process. (He grumbled at the time, but it has been easier ever since!)

Another common outdoor decorating idea is the use of greenery. Wreaths, pine cones, pine boughs, garlands, and gilded fruit are all beautiful outdoor decorations. One family I know even planted a large pine tree in their front yard and decorate it as their main Christmas tree each year; then they can enjoy its beauty both indoors and outdoors.

Other people focus on a specific style. Some purchase or build large scale scenes to put on their rooftops or lawns. Still others add taped music to their outdoor decorations. You may want to do all of these or none of these, but whatever you decide to do, let your house look like Christmas!

68

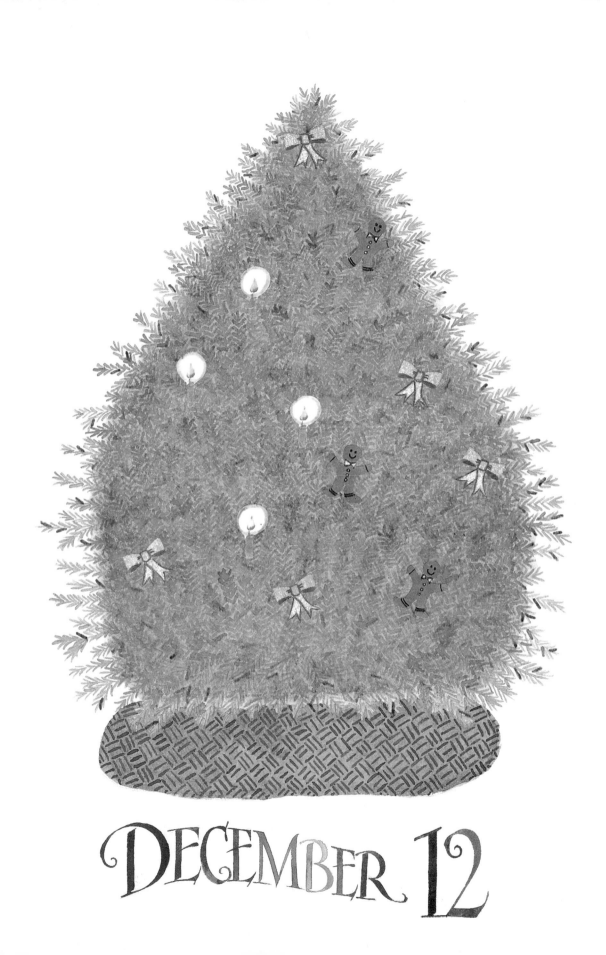

DECEMBER 12

Mary and Joseph came into Bethlehem hot and dusty and tired from their long journey. Mary's baby was ready to come and they needed a place to stay. So they went to the most logical place—a motel or inn. But Bethlehem was so crowded with people coming into town to be taxed that the inns were all filled. Mary and Joseph were worried. They needed a place for their baby to be born!

And God provided one. It wasn't in a comfortable hotel or someone's house. It wasn't in a huge palace where you might think the Son of God should be born.

Everyone would like to go to a palace. It's beautiful and has gorgeous paintings and valuable furniture. But you can't just walk right into a palace. You have to be a very important person or a friend of the king to be able to go to a palace. You have to pass an inspection to make sure you aren't sneaking something in that will hurt the king. Then there are guards all over the palace who protect the king and who make sure that no one goes in an area that is off-limits.

Instead, Jesus was born in a stable—a place that isn't very comfortable or nice. A stable is dirty. And you don't have to be anybody special to be able to go into a stable. Anyone can go there.

That is the lesson that God wants us to learn: He wants us to know that Jesus will go anywhere and that you don't have to be anyone super important or famous or rich to be able to come to Him. Jesus wants you. And He will do whatever He has to do to be able to have you come to Him—even be born in a dirty, stinky stable.

What is the hard situation that you're facing right now? Maybe school is hard for you, or maybe there is a bully at school who constantly teases you. Maybe your baseball team is the league champs this year . . . or the underdogs. Both of those extremes require strength of character to deal with in a sportsmanlike way. Maybe you just can't remember your times tables. What if you really blew it on the final unit test? Or what if your project partner is a lazy student who doesn't help get very much of the work done? What will you do?

No matter what happens on any day, remember that Jesus is always there with you. When you don't know what to do, pray and ask Him to come *right then* and show you what to do. And He will . . . because Jesus will go anywhere that you are!

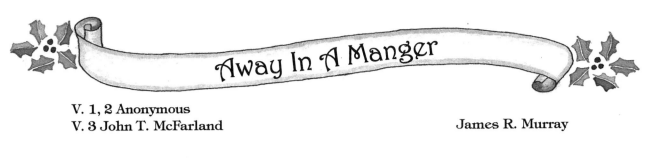

Away In A Manger

V. 1, 2 Anonymous
V. 3 John T. McFarland

James R. Murray

1. A - way in a man - ger, No crib for a bed, The lit - tle Lord
2. The cat - tle are low - ing, The Ba - by a - wakes, But lit - tle Lord
3. Be near me, Lord Je - sus, I ask Thee to stay Close by me for -

Je - sus Laid down His sweet head; The stars in the sky — Looked
Je - sus, No cry - ing He makes; I love Thee, Lord Je - sus! Look
ev - er, And love me, I pray; Bless all the dear chil - dren In

down where He lay, The lit - tle Lord Je - sus, A - sleep on the hay.
down from the sky, And stay by my cra - dle, Till morn - ing is nigh.
Thy ten - der care, And take us to heav - en, To live with Thee there.

One morning recently, I was thinking about my daughter and was overwhelmed with thankfulness for her. Later in the day, she walked into the room where I was. I turned to her and said, "Lindsey, this morning I was thinking about you and it made me so happy that I just wanted to get you and hold you for a long time." She looked me right in the eye and said, "Well, why don't you?" So I did!

This incident brought back to mind something that a woman in our congregation had shared with our women's group. She was studying for a degree in marriage and family counseling and was learning about the importance of touch. In her studies she had read that for a child to survive, he or she needs 4 loving touches per day; for that child to grow, he or she needs 8 loving touches per day; and for the child to flourish, he or she needs 12 loving touches per day.

Our group of ladies decided that we would each make a conscious effort to give each of our children 12 loving touches each day. In my case, that involved 36 loving touches because I have three children. I was surprised throughout the following week how difficult it was to meet that goal! But as time went on, I got better at it and my children began to respond to me with more loving touches of their own!

The abrupt words of my daughter made me realize that perhaps I was slipping in that area. It also made me realize how much the children still need my touches, even as big as they're getting.

That day she and I went in the family room with a video of her choice and I held her through an entire feature length movie! I've made an additional effort to caress the children's arms as I walk by, or brush their hair back from their faces as they're talking to me. Each morning when they wake up I try to greet each of them with a *long* hug and a kiss on the cheek. I hold their hands when we walk places together, I put my arm around their shoulders when we sit together. I haven't counted lately, so I don't know if I'm reaching the goal of 12 loving touches per child per day, but I think I'm doing pretty well!

Maybe this month, you'd like to hold your children for a while as you listen to their favorite Christmas tape, or hold hands on a walk, or give them extra hugs for no reason at all! What better time is there to express our love for one another, than at this time of year when we celebrate God sending His love-gift to the world. . . . And who knows—it might just become a habit!

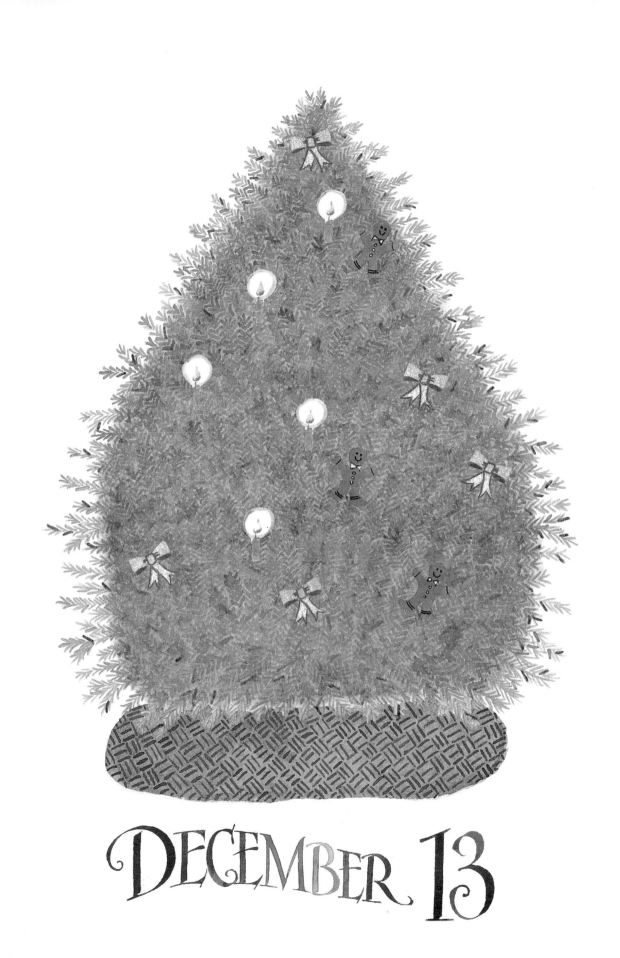

DECEMBER 13

Do your mom and dad have a special name they call you? My dad used to call me "Punkin," and I have lots of special names for my kids—probably five or six for each of them! But did you know that Father God is the same way with His Son, Jesus? There are over 300 names for Jesus listed in the Bible! It calls Him "Almighty" because there is nothing greater than Him. He is called the "Bread of Life" because He fills us, the "Door" because He is the way to God, the "Lamb of God" because He died for our sins, and the "Rock" because He is steady and unchanging. But one of the names that you hear a lot at Christmastime and in Christmas songs is Emmanuel, and it has a very special meaning. It means "God with us."

Before Jesus came, it was hard for people to know God. Of all the people in the world, only the Israelites knew about Him, and even they could only come to Him once a year. Only the priest was allowed to go into the holiest place one time each year to ask forgiveness for the whole nation.

But God made it possible for each person to come to Him by sending Jesus. John 1:14 says, "And the Word [Jesus] became flesh and dwelt among us." Jesus became a man so that we could see with our eyes what God was like. In John 14:9 Jesus said, "If you've seen Me, then you've seen the Father!" Jesus was someone we could touch and know. He was there with us. We could talk to Him whenever we wanted to! And because we know Jesus, we now know what God is like.

Isn't that an exciting thought? We can *know* God. He can be as close to us as our best friend. He knows us better than any one else! The Bible says that God cares so much about us, that He knows how many hairs we have on our heads (Luke 12:7), that He keeps each of our names before Him all the time (Isa. 49:16), and that *He is always with us!* (Heb. 13:5)

That's what Christmas is all about. Emmanuel: God is with us.

Thou Didst Leave Thy Throne

MARGARET

Emily E.S. Elliott

Timothy R. Matthews

1. Thou didst leave Thy throne And Thy king - ly crown When Thou
2. Heav - en's arch - es rang When the an - gels sang, Pro -
3. The __ fox - es found rest, And the birds their nest In the
4. Thou __ cam - est, O Lord, With the liv - ing word That should
5. When the heav - ens shall ring, And the an - gels sing, At Thy

cam - est to earth for me; But in Beth - le - hem's home
claim - ing Thy roy - al de - gree; But of low - ly birth
shade of the for - est tree; But Thy couch was the sod,
set Thy peo - ple free; But with mock - ing scorn,
com - ing to vic - to - ry, Let Thy voice call me home,

Was there found no room For Thy ho - ly na - tiv - i - ty:
Didst Thou come to earth, And in great - est hu - mil - i - ty;
O Thou Son of God, In the des - erts of Gal - i - lee:
And with crown of thorn, They bore Thee to Cal - va - ry;
Say - ing, "Yet there is room, There is room at My side for thee:"

Refrain

1-4. O come to my heart, Lord Je - sus, There is room in my heart for Thee.
5. My heart shall rejoice, Lord Je - sus, When Thou com - est and call - est for me.

75

Getting your annual batch of Christmas cards in the mail can be one of the most tedious jobs of the holidays. The repetition of signing, stamping, and sealing envelopes can all be a real test of patience. Yet there are ways to make it a family project.

First, get your Christmas cards together and devise a plan. Divide your cards up and do a few each night. Or write your family letter tonight, copy it tomorrow, and then have a marathon card stuffing evening. Try using an assembly line approach with each family member responsible for a different part of the job: Mom signs the cards, Susie puts them in the envelopes, Joey put on a stamp, and Dad addresses them. I like to divide the job by task: write and copy the Christmas letter one day, sign all of the cards one day, stamp the envelopes one day, etc.

In any event, the children can help by sealing envelopes, attaching return address stickers, and putting on stamps. Older children may even be able to address the envelopes. Involve the youngest children even if all they can do is hand you one envelope at a time for you to address. Don't tax their willingness to help, however. A toddler's interest in the job may only last for five envelopes. And make sure they wash their hands first (believe me, I've learned that one by experience!).

Another way the children can help is by putting together a Family Newspaper to put in each card. Have them write about their favorite event of the year, draw a pen and ink drawing to go along with it, and then sign their names. This gives long distance relatives an opportunity to see some of each child's personality. If your children are younger, you could write the letter, while having them tell you what they want to say.

When my husband and I were first married, the cost of postage and cards was about a third of what it is now. But now, as then, I think it's a good relational investment. I couldn't possibly afford to send each of those people a gift; but when I compute the cost of mailing each individual card, it seems a small price to pay to let far away friends and relatives know that they are always in my heart.

CHRISTMAS COUNTDOWN
· · · · · · · · · · · · ·

Now we're in the thick of things! Keep a running list of errands you need to run, and get them out of the way by using "time bytes." You could run a couple of errands during your lunch hour. Take advantage of the time during your son's basketball practice or your daughter's gymnastics class. Another great time for errand-running is right after dropping the children off at school—the stores are still relatively empty at that time, and you're "out and about" anyway.

*"If your parents
know how to give
you good gifts,
just think how much more
your Father God
will give good gifts
to those who ask!"*

Matthew 7:11

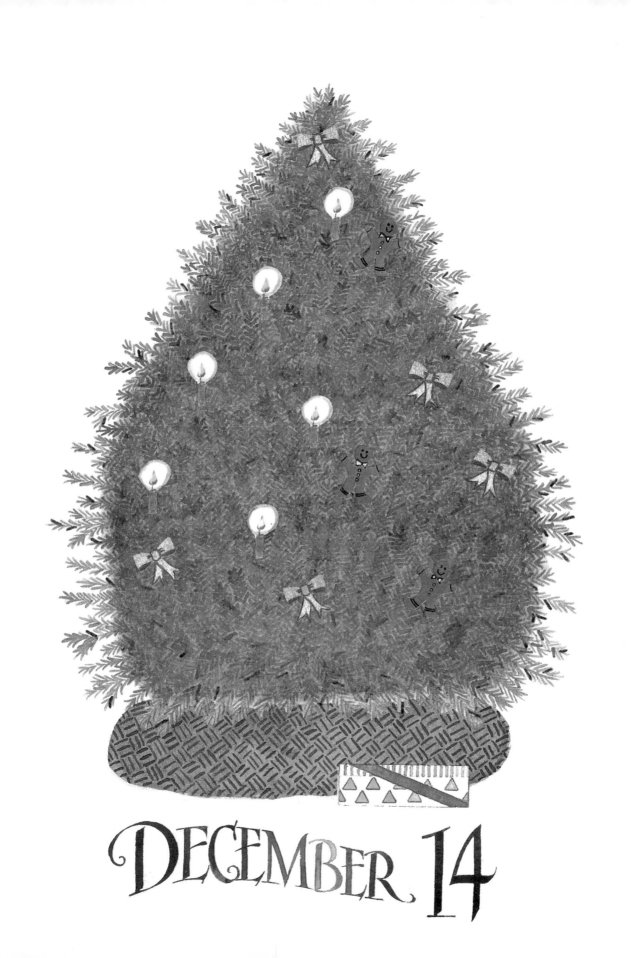

DECEMBER 14

When I was a little girl I heard someone say that our spirits were hungry for God. I wasn't sure what that meant, but I decided that it must be kind of the same as our bodies being hungry for food. When I got older, I found out that was exactly what it was like!

There is a place inside each of us that can't be filled up with food. You may think that when you eat it fills up all the places inside of you. But food can't fill up your spirit. We can't fill it up with soup and cereal and sandwiches; we have to fill it up with God. God made us to need Him, and if we don't include Him in our lives, then our spirits become hungry for Him.

When God created the first people, they were filled with God; but when they sinned, their spirits became empty and hungry for God. Ever since then, people have been trying to fill the hunger and emptiness in their spirits. And because God loves us, He made it possible for everyone to be filled with Him again.

God sent His Son, Jesus, to fill the empty place inside of us so that our spirits could be filled with God again. But to have that happen, we have to ask Jesus to come into our life. Remember that Jesus said that He was the Bread of Life? (John 6:48) He was saying that He knows our hearts are hungry and that He can fill them up, just like bread fills our stomachs.

Jesus, the Bread of Life, was born in a place called Bethlehem. Bethlehem actually means "the house of bread," or a bakery. What do we get from a bakery? (Bread.) What did God give us from Bethlehem—His bakery—that would fill our hungry hearts? (Jesus.) Just like we fill our bodies with food, we fill our spirits with Jesus, the Bread of Life.

Have you asked Jesus to come into your life? If you haven't, ask Him today. He wants to come live with you and fill your spirit with His bread—Jesus—so that your heart will never be hungry again.

Let Us Break Bread Together

Traditional Spiritual

1. Let us break bread to-geth-er on our knees;___
2. Let us drink the cup to-geth-er on our knees;___
3. Let us praise God to-geth-er on our knees;___

___ Let us break bread to-geth-er on our knees.___
___ Let us drink the cup to-geth-er on our knees.___
___ Let us praise God to-geth-er on our knees.___

When I fall on my knees; With my face to the ris-ing

sun, O___ Lord have mer-cy on - me.___

Many things that are incorporated into our celebration at Christmas are both symbolic and prophetic. They remind us of the Old Testament promises regarding the coming of the Messiah. They symbolize Jesus' actual coming, reminding us that Jesus "made Himself of no reputation, taking the form of a servant, and coming in the likeness of men" (Phil. 2:7). What a miracle! What a cause for rejoicing and celebration!

But Jesus' birth can never be separated from His death and resurrection. Neither would have significance without the other; and Jesus provided us with the ultimate visual aid to help our children grasp the relationship between the two when He instituted the Lord's Table. While it does give us an opportunity to explain the sacrifice of Jesus' body, it goes way beyond that! At this time of year, the bread can be used to portray how Jesus took on human flesh to live with all of mankind (John 1:14). And the wine, as a symbol of the Holy Spirit, becomes representative of the fact that not only did He come to "dwell among us" but to dwell within us (Rev. 3:20).

Use this opportunity to teach your children the guidelines found in 1 Corinthians 11:17-26. This isn't a time merely to mourn again over the fact that Jesus had to die, although a certain sobriety and reverence are always appropriate. But "Do this in remembrance of Me" is a call to rejoice in all that Jesus has done for us in providing salvation and forgiveness and healing. And, yes, all of that was provided for us because of His death on the cross. But Jesus doesn't call us to live in grief any more than a beloved relative who died would wish for us to dwell only on the fact that they are gone. The Lord's Table gives us an opportunity to celebrate the triumph of the cross, not just mourn over the fact of the cross.

As you serve the Lord's Table to your family, don't feel disqualified. Scripture (1 Peter 2:9; Rev. 5:10) says that we have been made a nation of kings and priests unto our God. However, if you do feel hesitant to serve Communion yourself, plan to participate in Communion together as a family sometime at church this month. In either case, allow a spirit of joy and reverence to fill your home and hearts as you rejoice together in God's greatest gift to each of us.

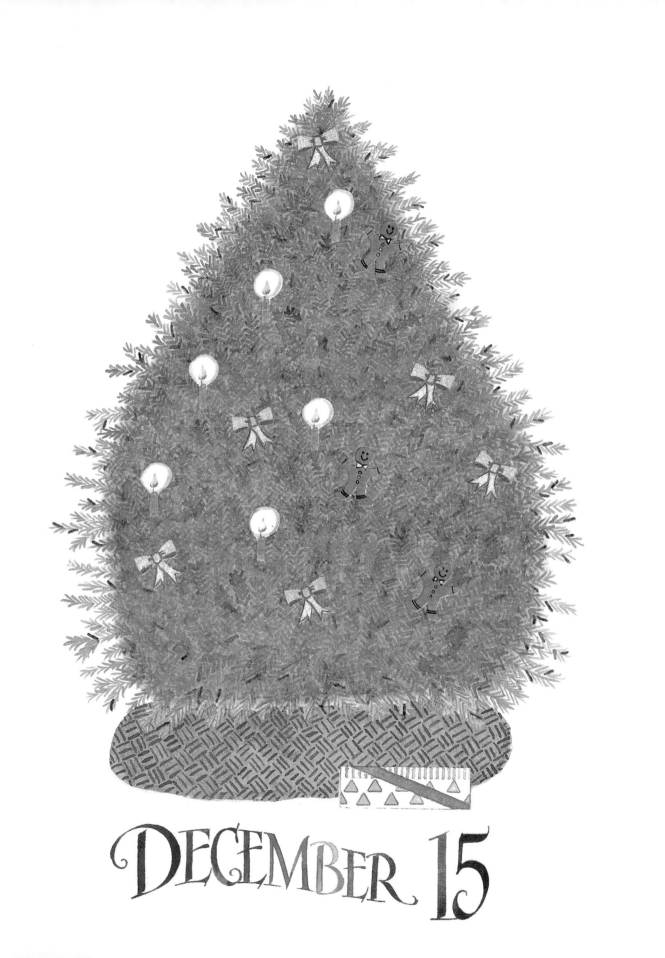

DECEMBER 15

Christmas is called a time of peace. People talk about it. You've probably seen doves or other kinds of peace symbols on Christmas cards. But what most people don't talk about is *why* this is a season of peace.

When the angels announced Jesus' birth, they sang, "Peace on earth!" because one of the names for the promised Savior was the "Prince of Peace" (Isa. 9:6). They were proclaiming that Peace had now come to rule on earth! Many people thought that meant that as soon the Messiah came, He would "protect all the good guys and get rid of all the bad guys (or maybe throw them in jail)" like some kind of cartoon super hero! But Jesus came to bring a different kind of peace. He gives us a peace that stays with us no matter what. God's kind of peace fills your heart and makes you feel loved. It is a peace that only God can give and there is nothing else that can take its place.

Many people try to fill that place with something else. Do you know kids who are angry and bully other kids? They are trying to fill that place with power. Some kids try to fill that place with friends, or food, or lots of toys and clothes. They are trying to fill that place with acceptance. Other kids try to fill that God-shaped place with something good like getting good grades, or being helpful. But even if you try filling that place in your heart with good things, it will be like using the wrong key in a lock. It can never open the door to God's peace, and will never make you completely happy, because you have tried to fill it with something that doesn't fit right.

Have you ever tried to open a door with the wrong key? It might look like the right key. It might even go into the lock. But when you try to turn it and open the door, nothing happens. That is what it's like when we try to fill our hearts with something other than God: we become frustrated, unhappy, and upset. But when we fill our hearts with the Lord, we find peace.

Jesus said, "In Me you may have peace. In the world you will have hard things happen to you; but be of good cheer, I have conquered the world" (John 16:33).

That means that no matter what difficult situation we face, we can have peace. If you aren't facing something hard right now, thank the Lord. But if you are, ask the Lord to help you, talk to your mom or dad, and remember: No matter what you face, the Prince of Peace is right there with you.

What Child Is This?

William C. Dix

GREENSLEEVES
English Melody

1. What Child is this, who, laid to rest, On Mary's lap is sleeping? Whom angels greet with anthems sweet, While shepherds watch are keeping?
2. Why lies He in such mean estate, Where ox and ass are feeding? Good Christian, fear for sinners here The silent Word is pleading.
3. So bring Him incense, gold and myrrh, Come, rich and poor, to own Him; The King of kings, salvation brings, Let loving hearts enthrone Him.

Refrain

This, this is Christ the King, Whom shepherds guard and angels sing: Haste, haste to bring Him laud, The Babe, the Son of Mary.

December is a great birthday month! When our oldest son was born in December, it gave me a whole new outlook on Christmas: a new understanding of the practical things Mary went through (can you imagine riding on a donkey when you're nine months pregnant?), of the travail that had to take place so that God's gift could be given to us, and of the awe of seeing a new life brought into the world.

But on the other hand, the busyness of the season can mean that a December birthday can inadvertently be set aside or lost in the holiday hustle and bustle. I've heard "December-birthday" people complain about no party, no celebration, sometimes even no gifts because their birthday gifts would be combined with their Christmas gifts.

If you have a family member whose birthday is this month, plan to make it an extra special day. On our kids' birthdays we always tell the story of the day they were born. They hear about funny things that were said, how long it took, the exact minute they were born, and how happy we were to have them. And we always remind them, "I'm glad that you were born, and I'm glad that Jesus gave you to me."

But because this is a December birthday, we do a few things that are different. We try to coordinate some of our traditions as a family with Brian's birthday. First, because our evening schedule in December is usually so packed, we'll celebrate his birthday and open gifts at breakfast. We will either have a special breakfast at home or go early (before school) to a restaurant with a breakfast smorgasbord. We will also usually buy and decorate our Christmas tree that day.

But there are tons of other ideas for December birthdays! Maybe go caroling and sing happy birthday at every house. Or plan something totally zany for a party . . . one year our son Kyle wanted to color eggs at his birthday party—it didn't matter that the birthday wasn't anywhere near Easter! Maybe a special Christmas tree or snowman shaped birthday cake is what your child would like to accompany their favorite dinner. Or you could all wear Santa hats at the birthday party! Whatever you choose to do, make the day special so that your birthday boy or girl knows that you are glad that they were born!

Even if there isn't someone in your family having a birthday this month, we all know Someone whose birthday IS this month! Maybe a birthday party for Jesus would be a good reminder for us all of the joy that was in Father God's heart at Jesus' birth. I'm glad that He was born . . . aren't you?

CHRISTMAS COUNTDOWN

• • • • • • • • • • • •

All of your Christmas cards should be in
the mail by today.

"Receive the
gift of the
Holy Spirit."

Acts 2:38

DECEMBER 16

There are lots of bells around at Christmas! We sing "Jingle Bells" or "Silver Bells." At church we might hear, "I Heard the Bells on Christmas Day." People hang bells on their doors and Christmas trees. And there are whole strings of bells on street decorations and window displays.

In our country, bells are important because the Liberty Bell is a well-known symbol of freedom. Did you know that it even has a Bible verse on it? It has Leviticus 25:10, which says, "Proclaim liberty throughout all the land to all its inhabitants." So that whenever that bell was rung it was supposed to remind people that they were free.

While the Bible doesn't say much about bells, it *does* teach us about freedom and that true freedom comes only through Jesus. That is why He came—so that He could make us free. The Bible says that wherever the Lord is there is freedom (2 Cor. 3:17). That means that if we've asked Jesus into our hearts and He lives in us, we can be free!

Just like the Israelites were slaves in Egypt, the devil wants to make us slaves by convincing us that wrong things are OK to do. You might decide to tell a lie. Or you might cheat on a test at school. Or you might steal a candy bar from the market. But it is *always* a trick. What the devil wants to do is trap you into a habit that you can't stop . . . so that you become a slave to lying or cheating or stealing.

Here's how it happens: Ask Mom to wrap one string of thread around you. You can break that pretty easily, can't you? And if she wraps five or six strings of thread around you, you could probably break it, but it would be a little harder. But if she wrapped nineteen or twenty threads around you, you probably couldn't break it at all.

Every time you give in to doing something wrong, Satan wraps a string around you. It may not seem like very much at first, but if you continue doing it and he continues wrapping strings around you it will become a habit you can't break. And if there's something in your life that you can't stop, then you have become a slave to that. You aren't free anymore.

The good news is that if Jesus has made you free, you're really free (John 8:36). There's no question about it! Because Jesus came (which is what we're celebrating now), died for us, and rose again, He has the power to break all the strings that are around us!

So whenever you hear a bell—a sleigh bell, a church bell, a Salvation Army bell, even a doorbell!—remember that Jesus came to make us free, not just in our country, but in our hearts.

I Heard The Bells On Christmas Day

Henry W. Longfellow

Jean Baptiste Calkin

1. I heard the bells on Christ-mas day Their old fa-mil-iar
2. I thought how, as the day had come, The bel-fries of all
3. And in de-spair I bowed my head: "There is no peace on
4. Yet pealed the bells more loud and deep: "God is not dead, nor
5. Then ring-ing, sing-ing on its way, The world re-volved from

car-ols play, And wild and sweet the words re-peat Of
Chris-ten-dom Had rolled a-long th'un-bro-ken song Of
earth," I said, "For hate is strong, and mocks the song Of
doth He sleep; The wrong shall fail, the right pre-vail, With
night to day— A voice, a chime, a chant sub-lime Of

Optional transition to "Come On, Ring Those Bells"

peace on earth, good will to men.
peace on earth, good will to men.
peace on earth, good will to men."
peace on earth, good will to men."
peace on earth, good will to men! will to men!

faster

Christmas vacation has started! And while you may have more to do than the hours of the day allow, time hangs heavy on your kids' hands! Help the children to use this time constructively! When our kids are home, we encourage them to read, draw, and play outdoors. But we also have them work on projects that benefit the whole family.

One day off of school, my kids were surprised to find out that I planned for them to sand and prime the garage door so that Daddy could paint it after work! You may not want to take on that ambitious of a project, but there is always yard work to be done and even mundane jobs like raking leaves can take on a new look when you do them together . . . and promise hot apple cider for a job well done!

Let the children help you with the housework. By the age of ten, each of my children could clean the bathrooms, vacuum, and mop floors (almost) as well as I could. Not only has it helped them learn the importance of working together as a family (as well as mastering some very important college survival skills!), but it has been a huge help to me in weeks that are unbelievably busy. I've also found that they can straighten and organize their own closets and dresser drawers pretty well on a particularly "boring" day!

Make a batch of salt-flour dough and let the kids make ornaments, small figurines, or even a nativity! Between the making, drying, and painting, they'll have a nice-sized project on their hands. Or plan a project that uses fabric. Let the kids color a tree skirt made from a sheet. Give them fabric paints and let them use their imagination. Or have them decorate T-shirts for different members of the family. Any of these would be great gifts as well as being a fun project.

DECEMBER 17

hen I think of Christmas, I think of angels! They are mentioned in Christmas carols. We put them on the tops of our Christmas trees. They are on Christmas cards. And they are in the nativity sets that we put on the mantel over the fireplace or on tables specially decorated in honor of Jesus' birthday.

Angels *do* play a big part in the story of Jesus' birth. Throughout the Christmas story, angels bring messages to quite a few people. In fact, the word "angel" means "messenger." An angel came to Mary to announce that she would be the mother of the Messiah. An angel told Joseph not to worry, that Mary's baby really was going to be the Savior. An angel warned the wise men not to go back to Herod. And we know that a whole choir of angels announced Jesus' birth to the shepherds.

But the angel's announcement to the shepherds didn't start out with a whole choir.

Throughout the Bible, every time God sent an angel with a message, only one angel came. But at Jesus' birth, a whole choir came! Some have even wondered if maybe all the angels of heaven were so excited about Jesus' birth and God's plan to save everyone, that they couldn't contain themselves. They just burst out into praise!

Like the angels, God wants us to be praisers and messengers too.

The Bible says that the Lord lives in the praises of His people (Ps. 22:3); when we praise the Lord, we're actually building a place so that the Lord can live with us! When we praise the Lord, it also helps us to "proclaim the praises of Him who called" us from darkness into light (1 Peter 2:9). Praise helps make us free (2 Chron. 20; Acts 16:25). Psalm 147:1 says, "It is good to sing praises to our God." And Jesus even said that through little children comes perfect praise (Matt. 21:16). He wants us to be praisers!

We are also to be messengers. Mark 16:15 says that Jesus commanded His followers to go to the whole world and give everyone God's message. If we are Jesus' followers, then He also wants us to give people His message. Sometimes we can be His messengers by telling people how to know the Lord. Other times we are His messengers by being kind and showing Jesus' love. Sometimes we are His messengers by praying for someone who is sad or sick or scared.

Let's decide today, that, like the angels, we will be God's praisers and God's messengers too.

Hark, the Herald Angels Sing

Felix Mendelssohn
Adapted by William H. Cummings

Charles Wesley

1. Hark, the her - ald an - gels sing, "Glo - ry to the new - born King;
2. Christ, by high-est heaven a - dored; Christ, the ev - er - last - ing Lord!
3. Hail, the heaven-born Prince of Peace! Hail, the Sun of Righteous - ness!

Peace on earth, and mer - cy mild, God and sin - ners rec - on - ciled!"
Late in time be - hold Him come, Off - spring of the vir - gin's womb.
Light and life to all He brings, Ris'n with heal - ing in His wings.

Joy - ful, all ye na - tions, rise, Join the tri - umph of the skies;
Veiled in flesh the God - head see; Hail th' in - car - nate De - i - ty,
Mild He lays His glo - ry by, Born that man no more may die.

With th' an - gelic host pro - claim, "Christ is born in Beth - le - hem!"
Pleased as man with men to dwell, Je - sus, our Em - man - u - el!
Born to raise the sons of earth, Born to give them se - cond birth.

Hark, the her - ald an - gels sing, "Glo - ry to the new - born King."

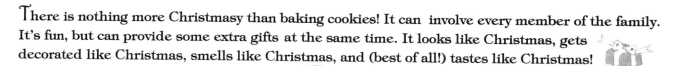

Cookies

There is nothing more Christmasy than baking cookies! It can involve every member of the family. It's fun, but can provide some extra gifts at the same time. It looks like Christmas, gets decorated like Christmas, smells like Christmas, and (best of all!) tastes like Christmas!

Involve the children by letting them help choose recipes, get out ingredients, measure, put away ingredients, stir, lick spoons, cut out cookies, lick fingers, grease cookie sheets, put cookies on cookie sheets, lick bowls, wash bowls, and decorate.

The only drawback to having the children help out is that their enthusiasm sometimes makes the mess bigger! So be prepared with an extra dose of patience and a sink full of soapy water so that fingers, bowls, and counters can be cleaned up quickly. My kids help by putting ingredients away as soon as they are measured out. This keeps the counters clear and spills at a minimum. I also have them wear old, oversized T-shirts in place of aprons to keep their clothes clean.

Cookie recipes like chocolate chip cookies and peanut butter cookies are quick and easy to make. (The store-bought tubes of cookie dough make this job even easier!) Or you could choose a recipe that's been handed down in your family or is traditional to your ethnic background. Make plum puddings, trifle, or scones if you come from a British background. Scandinavian countries make peppernut cookies, lace cookies, and aebleskiver. Magi cakes and torrone come from Italy. Mexico offers flan and sopapillas; France, mousse and tarts; and Germany, berlinkranzer and spritz wreath cookies. Go to the library and look up a little of the history of your family's background and give your children a history lesson plus a cooking lesson!

Along with those recipes, let your children try some "artistic" cookies. Make sugar cookies and let the kids cut them into shapes. (Encourage them to keep trying even if the cookie dough stretches and Rudolph comes out looking like a giraffe!) Then along with frosting and sprinkles, let them try painting their cookies. (Paint cookies before baking.) You can make cookie paint by combining an egg yolk and food coloring. Add a few drops of water as necessary for a good painting consistency. Then let them go for it!

Plates of cookies are always fun gifts to give and to receive. Make up a few to give to office staff, neighbors, and school teachers. You'll find that not only did you spread Christmas cheer when you made the cookies, but you spread more Christmas cheer when you gave them away!

CHRISTMAS COUNTDOWN

• • • • • • • • • • • • • • •

Call your local UPS office to find out
when is the last day to ship packages
anywhere in the continental United States
at their lowest rate.

"God has given
each one of us gifts,
and with these gifts
we are to bless
the people around us."

1 Peter 4:10

DECEMBER 18

Have you ever noticed that when you open a closet door, the room you're in doesn't get darker? Instead, the closet gets lighter! That's what the verse in John means when it says, "The light shines in the darkness; the darkness can never put it out!" (John 1:5, Simple English Bible) "The Light" that verse was talking about is Jesus! Jesus came to fill our hearts with light. And He promises that if you will open the door of your heart to Him, He will come in and make it light! He will do for us exactly what happened with the closet.

Before Jesus came, the world was in total darkness. That doesn't mean there was no sunshine, but that people's hearts were dark with sin and there was no light to show them how to find God.

Before Jesus came, there were no pastors or missionaries. There were priests and prophets, but they taught that someday the Messiah—the Savior—would come and help them find God again. Then into this darkness, Jesus was born.

The Bible calls Jesus the Light of the world. *He* is the Messiah that the prophets said would come someday. *He* is the One who would give us a light to find our way back to God. If you're lost and can't find your way, what do you use to find your way around? A light! That's why God sent Jesus and called Him a light . . . so that Jesus could help us find God and not be "lost in the darkness of sin" any more.

When we put lights on our house and Christmas tree, or put candles around the house at Christmastime, it's to remind us that Jesus came to be our light. The next time you're driving around and you see a Christmas tree or some beautiful lights on a house, you'll know why they're there! Because Jesus is the Light of the world!

The Light Has Come

Jack W. Hayford   Jack W. Hayford

1. The Light has come and the dark-ness can nev-er be the same, O hal-le-
2. The sound of joy fills the earth and sky and the bells peal forth their hal-le-
3. A sil-ver beam splits the sky a-bove and His star ap-pears, O hal-le-
4. The Light has come and for ev-'ry man Life has come to light, O hal-le-

lu - jah! The light has shown and the dark-ness ran nev-er to re-turn. O hal-le-
lu - jah! The day has dawned and the sun climbs high, for the Light has come. O hal-le-
lu - jah! A glo-ry streams spread-ing hope and love as Mes-si-ah comes, O hal-le-
lu - jah! Tho' some re-sist it, they nev-er can o-ver-come its pow'r. O hal-le-

lu! Thy Word made flesh, Thy Glo-ry re-vealed; its en-trance gave great
lu! This child now born, Him-self is the truth; the Truth which sets men
lu! He tramp-les dark-ness un-der His feet, His bat-tle flag un-
lu! For God in flesh once walked on the earth as Je-sus, Son of

light. You spoke, He came; Christ Je-sus His Name. And He has scat-tered our
free. His glo-ry shines to all of man-kind and His light brings lib-er-
furled; Des-pair and bond-age shat-ter and flee, for He's the light of the
Man. The splen-dor of His glo-ry dis-played con-tin-ues ag-es to

night. The Light has come and the dark-ness can nev-er be the same. O hal-le-
ty. The sound of joy fills the earth and sky and the bells peal forth their hal-le-
world. A sil-ver beam splits the sky a-bove and His star ap-pears. O hal-le-
span. The Light has come and to ev-'ry man Life has been re-vealed. O hal-le-

lu - jah! And now the Light shines to ev-'ry man. You can live in light, O hal-le-lu!
lu - jah! With free-dom's song lift your voice and cry, Je-sus Christ is Lord, O hal-le-lu!
lu - jah! His king-dom come is a rule of love cast-ing out all fear, O hal-le-lu!
lu - jah! And as it shines un-to me I can be re-newed in life, O hal-le-lu!

This evening, give the children a visual picture of what you read about today. Turn out all the lights in your house and see how dark it is. Then light just one candle. It's amazing how much light one candle throws! Then turn on the Christmas tree and light any other candles you may have around the house. The room will turn into a shimmering, glowing dwelling place of light. It's beautiful!

Or go out and look at Christmas lights! My favorite way to do this is with all the car windows down. I guess it's my "city version" of a sleigh! Bundle everybody up, provide bags of popcorn, and enjoy looking at lights, eating popcorn, and singing every Christmas carol you can think of! And, if it's cold enough, you may want to consider a cup of hot chocolate before bed.

The Jewish celebration of Hanukkah is another way to celebrate the coming of the Light. Hanukkah is also called the Festival of Lights and much of the celebration centers around the lighting of the menorah each of the eight nights. The candles stand for courage, justice, and hope and the commemoration itself stems from a period in history when the Jews not only faced extermination, but were being forced to worship pagan gods. Through the leadership of the priests, God worked mightily in their behalf, and they miraculously triumphed! (Check the library for more information on this meaningful observance.)

Let the kids share again what they've learned about Jesus being the Light of the world, and have a family candle-lighting, symbolizing not only the coming of Jesus but the overflow of His life into your family and home. It's a simple, yet powerful picture of what Jesus came to do!

DECEMBER 19

Some people put a big, bright bow on top of their Christmas tree. Other people put a beautiful angel. We put a star on our tree. We chose to put that instead of one of the other things because we wanted to remind ourselves that everything about the Christmas celebration is supposed to point to Jesus. That is what the star did at the first Christmas . . . it pointed the wise men to Jesus!

The Bible also says that "Star" is another name for Jesus! Moses prophesied in Numbers 24:17, that "a Star shall come out of Jacob." And in Revelation 22:16, Jesus Himself said, "I am . . . the Bright and Morning Star."

Sometimes people put stars in too important of a place. Just like in the Christmas story, where there was an actual star that guided people to Jesus and a Person who was called a star, there is the same thing today. There are people we call "stars" on TV or in movies, but they don't shine like Jesus. Some people rely on the stars in the sky to show them how to manage their lives. But the stars can't tell you what to do with your life! Not the ones on TV or the ones in the sky.

Scripture says that while nature is beautiful, its *purpose* is to point us to the Lord (Rom. 1:20). The psalmist talks to God saying, "When I consider Your heavens, the work of Your fingers, the moon and the stars, which You have ordained, what is man that You are mindful of him, and the son of man that You visit him?" (8:3-4) In other words, he asks, "When I see Your majesty displayed in creation, O Lord, why would You bother with me?" Yet God has poured out His love on us: and the stars are to help point us to the Creator.

Other people turn to people who are called "stars"—movie stars or rock stars. Sometimes they make these people so important in their lives, that they become more important than God. Yet Scripture reminds us many times that no one can compare to the Lord! No one else, no matter how captivating or attention-getting, can complete us like the Lord can.

Then as we follow Jesus, who is the Bright and Morning Star, He lights our path! Second Peter 1:19 tells us that as we walk in Jesus' light it causes "the morning star [to rise] in our hearts," so that as we continue to walk in God's light, our hearts grow bigger to love Him more every day. I want that in my life. Don't you?

Go, Tell It On The Mountain

Traditional Spiritual

Go, tell it on the moun - tain, O - ver the hills and ev - 'ry-where;

Fine

Go, tell it on the moun - tain That Je - sus Christ is born.

1. While shep-herds kept their watch-ing O'er si - lent flocks by night, Be -
2. The shep-herds feared and trem-bled When, lo! a bove tho earth Rang
3. Down in a low - ly man - ger Our hum-ble Christ was born, And

D. C.

hold, through-out the heav-ens There shone a ho - ly light.
out the an - gel cho - rus That hailed our Sav - ior's birth.
God sent us sal - va - tion That bless - ed Christ-mas morn.

105

Living in Southern California, my children have not had a lot of experience with freezing winters or snow. If we get one morning of frost it's a novelty and we all run outside to look at the white roofs! But even at this young age they have discovered that in our culture, "Christmas" and "snow" go together. They see it on Christmas cards, TV specials, and decorations. And even though they know virtually nothing about it, they LOVE it. In fact *every* kid seems to love snow!

So plan some time this month to take a break and have a special snow outing, whether that time is a short hour and a half after work one night or an all-day weekend event. You may live in a climate like we do where you can go to the snow for an afternoon. One year, our "snow day" took a total of four hours. We drove to some nearby mountains and went sledding, ate an icicle, built a snowman, and threw a few snowballs. By then the kids were cold enough to go home!

If you live in an already-cold climate where snow doesn't carry the novelty that it does in Los Angeles, try something totally different: clear off that picnic table and eat a (quick) dinner of chili, cornbread, and hot cocoa or apple cider! The neighbors may think you're crazy, but I guarantee you that your children won't forget it! Top your evening off by watching a Christmas video together in front of a roaring fire.

Even if you live in a desert climate, you can do something related to snow. Some places "import" or make snow that can be enjoyed during the Christmas season. I've even seen some families spray paint tumbleweeds white and build a desert-style snowman! Or maybe make your own snow in the form of homemade ice cream!

Maybe the extent of your snow day will be to add to your Christmas decorations. You could set up a snow scene decoration on the dining room table. Maybe cut out cotton to put on your window sills to create a snow effect. Or use this day to put "snow" on your Christmas tree.

DECEMBER 20

This month you've read about the connection between the gift of Jesus' coming at Christmas, and the gift of our salvation at Easter. But another connection between the two of them can be seen in the colors of Christmas.

The colors most often used are red, green, gold, and white. We use those colors in our decorations and in the clothes we wear. Those colors burst out in stores and street decorations and Christmas cards. It seems that in December, the whole world has turned red and green! And there is a natural explanation as to why we use those colors.

The red and green comes from the plants that are living at this time of year: evergreen trees, holly with its bright red berries, and poinsettias. White, of course, is from the snow that covers much of our country in the winter. And gold not only is one of the gifts that the wise men brought to Baby Jesus, but it is also a color that belongs to a king—which Jesus is. Besides, gold is just a fun color to celebrate with because it's bright, shiny, and happy!

But the Bible talks about colors too and in them we again see the story of our salvation.

Isaiah 1:18 promises that "though your sins be as scarlet, they shall be white as snow." It's a perfect picture of what Jesus did for us: He has forgiven us of our sins; He has washed us so that we are now clean and pure before God (see Ps. 51:7). God also promises to clothe His people in white garments. Revelation 7:14 says that the saints "washed their robes and made them white in the blood of the Lamb."

Then, because we have been made clean through Jesus' blood, God makes us like a green tree that lives forever before Him. Jeremiah 17:7-8 says, "Blessed is the one who trusts in the Lord, and whose hope is the Lord. For he shall be like a tree planted by the waters, which spreads out its roots by the river. . . [its] leaf will be green . . . nor will [it] cease from yielding fruit." (See also 11:16.)

Finally, the Lord promises us a crown of gold because through Jesus, we too have become God's children! David sang about our salvation in Psalm 21:3 and said, "For You meet him [that's us!] with the blessings of goodness; You set a crown of pure gold upon his head." The Bible also uses gold to describe heaven (Rev. 21:18); our beliefs (1 Peter 1:7); and the Word of God (Ps. 19:10).

This Christmas as our celebrating fills you with joy, let the colors of our celebration also fill you with joy as they remind us of God's great gift to us through Jesus.

On This Christmas Day

Jack W. Hayford

Ash Grove
Traditional Welsh Melody

Lord Je-sus our Sav-ior the gift of the Fa-ther's fa-vor, ap-peared in a low-ly man-ger, on this Christ-mas Day. With car-ols loud-ly ring-ing, and bright voic-es glad-ly sing-ing, our praise joy-ous-ly we're bring-ing, on this Christ-mas Day. There is naught ev-er to com-pare with the love He has come to share with us; God come as man to bear with us all of our need. And thus the re-ve-la-tion of God's gra-cious sal-va-tion which themes all our ce-le-bra-tion on this Christ-mas Day.

Santa Claus is a uniquely American character. While his origins may stem from St. Nicholas (who is known as the patron saint of children), and the Dutch Sinter Klaas, Americans took him and made him completely their own. In the frontier days of the prairie and the far west, Santa Claus was even portrayed riding a pack mule!

But among believers, Santa Claus has become the subject of much controversy. And with good reason! Once the Bible and "religion" were thrown out of the school, there was no one else to focus on at Christmas. Santa Claus became the center of the season. People no longer greeted each other with "Merry Christmas," but with "Happy Holidays." "Getting" not "giving" was basic to the season as materialism took over. Of course, the merchants picked up on that and now Christmas decorations are out almost before school starts in September!

What is sad, however, is the fact that children have a natural inclination toward wanting to pretend—and, yes, even believe in these fantasy characters. From Mickey Mouse and Tony the Tiger to the pot of gold at the end of the rainbow, children want to believe in the magical. Personally, while I don't remember ever believing in Santa Claus, I honestly believed in wishing on a star! Fantasy is a part of childhood! And it is unfortunate that our society has forced us into a position of having to choose between the foundation of our faith and the enchantment of imagination.

But the question still remains: what do we do with Santa Claus? Many Christian parents fear that if their children grow up believing in Jesus *and* Santa Claus, that when they find out Santa Claus isn't real they will question the reality of Jesus as well. That can be a genuine dilemma for some people.

With our children, we decided to keep the fun of Santa at Christmastime. While the focus of our celebration has never been on Santa, we do go visit him at the mall, and my kids are still *sure* that they heard sleigh bells in the sky one year!

But we have always told them the truth. From their earliest years we told them that Santa Claus was pretend. They didn't listen to us because they wanted to believe that he was real! But as they got older and learned that he really was imaginary, they discovered something else: Mom and Dad had always told them the truth. About Santa Claus *and* about Jesus!

All of us, as Christians, are diligent to not let society rob Christmas of the holiday's true meaning; but neither should we allow it to rob us of the season's childlike fantasy!

CHRISTMAS COUNTDOWN

• • • • • • • • • • • • •

Even though this is the age of two-day
mail (a practical, albeit expensive,
convenience), you may want to allow
extra time for shipping's busiest month of
the year. Try to get any last-minute
packages in the mail today.

*"We have been saved
by believing in
Jesus Christ.
It's nothing that
we've done . . .
it is God's gift."*

Ephesians 2:8

DECEMBER 21

Jesus said that He came to be our Shepherd (John 10:11). In Israel, 2,000 years ago, that phrase probably didn't need very much explanation, because most people would have known someone who was a shepherd. They would have known what shepherds did. But not very many of *us* have met shepherds or been around flocks of sheep to understand what that means. So what does a shepherd do for his sheep that Jesus wants to do for us?

The Bible gives us a good idea of what shepherds do in the 23rd Psalm. It was written by David, who was also a shepherd. And David writes that shepherds do eight things:

The Lord is my shepherd; I shall not want. [The Shepherd provides for all the needs of the sheep.]

He makes me to lie down in green pastures; He leads me beside the still waters. He restores my soul. [He gives them safety and rest.]

He leads me in the paths of righteousness for His name's sake. [He leads the sheep.]

Yea, though I walk through the valley of the shadow of death, I will fear no evil; for You are with me; Your rod and Your staff [He protects the sheep], they comfort me. [The Shepherd comforts the sheep when they are afraid.]

You prepare a table before me in the presence of my enemies [He feeds the sheep, even in difficult situations]; You anoint my head with oil; My cup runs over. [The Shepherd pours oil on the sheep so their wounds can be healed.]

Surely goodness and mercy shall follow me all the days of my life; and I will dwell in the house of the Lord forever. [The Shepherd promises that the sheep will always be with Him.]

So Jesus, in saying that He wants to be *our* Shepherd, is telling us that He wants to do those things for us! How? He promises to provide everything we need. He feeds us when we read our Bibles. He comforts us when we're afraid and gives us peace by making His presence real to us. He helps us know where we're supposed to go and what we're supposed to do with our lives. He protects us. He heals us when we're sick in our bodies or hurt in our hearts. And He promises that He will live with us and never leave us alone.

Isn't it great to have Someone to do all of those things for you? Moms and Dads try, although they can't always be with us. But Jesus promises to always be with us. It's why He came!

Saviour, Like A Shepherd Lead Us

Dorothy A. Thrupp

Wm. B. Bradbury

1. Sav-iour, like a shep-herd lead us, Much we need Thy ten-der care;
2. We are Thine; do Thou be-friend us, Be the Guard-ian of our way;
3. Thou hast prom-ised to re - ceive us, Poor and sin-ful though we be;
4. Ear - ly let us seek Thy fa - vor; Ear-ly let us do Thy will;

In Thy pleas-ant pas-tures feed us, For our use Thy folds pre - pare:
Keep Thy flock, from sin de - fend us, Seek us when we go a - stray:
Thou hast mer-cy to re - lieve us, Grace to cleanse, and pow'r to free:
Bless - ed Lord and on - ly Sav - iour, With Thy love our bos-oms fill:

Bless - ed Je - sus, Bless-ed Je - sus, Thou hast bought us, Thine we are;
Bless - ed Je - sus, Bless-ed Je - sus, Hear Thy chil-dren when they pray;
Bless - ed Je - sus, Bless-ed Je - sus, Ear - ly let us turn to Thee;
Bless - ed Je - sus, Bless-ed Je - sus, Thou hast loved us, love us still;

Bless - ed Je - sus, Bless-ed Je - sus, Thou hast bought us, Thine we are.
Bless - ed Je - sus, Bless-ed Je - sus, Hear Thy chil-dren when they pray.
Bless - ed Je - sus, Bless-ed Je - sus, Ear - ly let us turn to Thee.
Bless - ed Je - sus, Bless-ed Je - sus, Thou hast loved us, love us still.

Have you ever made a gingerbread house with your kids? How about gingerbread men? In the middle of a hectic holiday month, it's nice to take an afternoon simply for doing something fun with the children. You need it and they need it. And even in the midst of a much-needed break, another project can be accomplished. An afternoon spent on a gingerbread house or gingerbread men can yield a dining room centerpiece or gifts for the neighbors. I realize that this sounds like a somewhat daunting project, but it doesn't have to be hard!

If you're home all day (this is me) and have tons of baking talent (this is not me), you might want to tackle a genuine gingerbread house! I tend to go an easier route on a project like this. Maybe some of these "quicker" versions will be better for you and provide just as much fun.

At Christmastime many markets and department stores carry gingerbread house kits that have everything prepared for you down to the last candy that goes on top of the chimney. All you have to do is put it together. Or you could make simple houses out of graham crackers and frosting. Try sticking the graham crackers to milk cartons for instant "houses," and build a whole village! My daughter doesn't want to even make houses . . . she just wants to decorate graham crackers. In a "technical" gingerbread house, everything must be edible. But if frosting is difficult for you to work with, use paste . . . just remember not to eat it!

Try building a log cabin out of candy cane sticks. Buy pre-made gingerbread men and let the kids stick on chocolate chip eyes and buttons. You could even make something as simple as marshmallow snowmen complete with toothpick arms and candy corn noses!

CHRISTMAS COUNTDOWN

• • • • • • • • • • • •

Only 4 shopping days left! But to make
your holiday as relaxed as possible, try
to have all of your shopping out of the
way today.

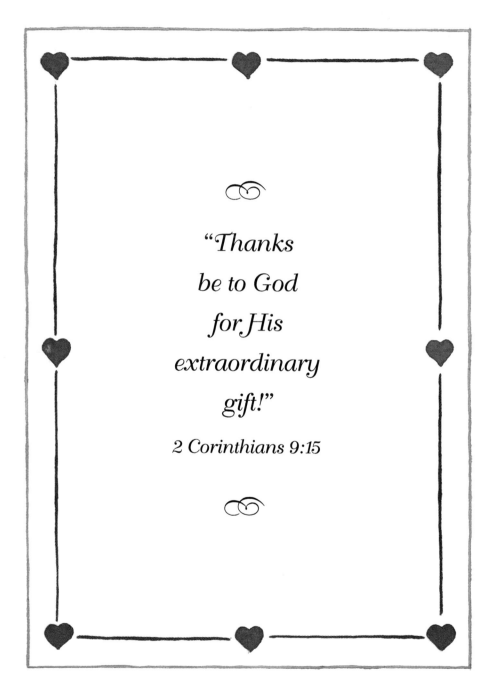

*"Thanks
be to God
for His
extraordinary
gift!"*

2 Corinthians 9:15

DECEMBER 22

Jesus once told a story about a lamb who was lost. He described a shepherd whose care for his sheep was so great that he searched for the one lost little sheep until he found it, even though he had a whole flock at home (Matt. 18:10-14; Luke 15:4-7).

We already learned that Jesus is called our Shepherd, and He cares for *us* in the same way. But this story describes one more thing that a shepherd does: he searches for his sheep. Jesus, as our Shepherd, does the same thing. He wants us to be His so much that He loves us and searches for us until He finds us.

On Christmas, we often think of the shepherds coming to find Baby Jesus. But *God* took the first step! God sent His angel to find the shepherds and tell them the good news of Jesus' birth. The shepherds are a picture for us to see God's heart: God wants us to hear the good news so much that He is willing to do whatever it takes to find each person.

The Bible says, "This is how God shows His love for us: while we were still sinners, He sent Jesus Christ to die for us" (Rom. 5:8). Once again, God took the first step! The Bible says that everyone has sinned, and that when you sin, you earn death (Rom. 3:23; 6:23). But the gift God sent to us in Jesus is *life*! (John 10:10)

It gets even better! First, God took the first step toward us, then He made His gift easy to receive! Acts 16:31 says, "Believe on the Lord Jesus Christ, and you will be saved." All the Lord asks us to do is believe that His gift is for us and that through Jesus our sins will be wiped away! Isn't that awesome? It's so simple! All you have to do to get God's gift is *receive it*!

When you do, the Bible tells us what will happen: "Now that we are set free from sin, and have become servants of God, the fruit [remember when we read about the ornaments?] of our lives will be holiness [wholeness, completeness], and we will also receive everlasting life" (Rom. 6:22).

Have you given your heart to Jesus? He is searching for you. He won't give up, either. He will search until He finds you. But now that you have heard the message, won't you, like the shepherds, come to Him and receive His gift? It's the best Christmas present you'll ever receive!

While Shepherds Watch Their Flocks

Nahum Tate

George Frederick Handel

1. While shep - herds watched their flocks by night, All seat - ed on
2. "Fear not!" said he; for might - y dread Had seized their troub -
3. "To you, in Da - vid's town this day, Is born of Da -
4. "The heav'n - ly Babe you there shall find To hu - man view
5. "All glo - ry be to God on high, And to the earth

the ground, The an - gel of the Lord came down,
led mind, "Glad ti - dings of great joy I bring
vid's line, The Sav - ior who is Christ the Lord,
dis - played, All mean - ly wrapped in swath - ing bands,
be peace: Good will hence - forth from heav'n to men,

And glo - ry shone a - round, And glo - ry shone a - round.
To you and all man - kind, To you and all man - kind.
And this shall be the sign: And this shall be the sign:
And in a man - ger laid; And in a man - ger laid.
Be - gin and nev - er cease, Be - gin and nev - er cease."

At our house, free evenings during the month of December are few and far between! You probably have the same hectic holiday schedule at your home. But occasionally an empty evening will pop up. Maybe you planned to leave the evening free. Or maybe something was canceled. Or maybe one of the children got the sniffles and just can't go out. Whatever the reason you're home tonight, use some of the time to spend with each other.

December has the advantage of presenting some of the best family TV of the year! There are almost always fun Christmas programs on that you can enjoy as a family. If nothing appeals to you there, you could rent a Christmas video. Or pull out the kids' favorite board game. My children will spend literally hours on a good rousing game of Monopoly (with a few made-up rules allowing for bank robbery, extra turns, and building houses on each other's property!).

One family I know reenacted the Christmas story together. They dressed up in old clothes, acted out the whole story (including using their pets as the animals), and took pictures of each other which they later put into a scrapbook as a Christmas memento!

However, with all of the exciting things to do at Christmastime, my children's favorite "free evening" event is still to make a huge bowl of popcorn, start a fire in the fireplace, and turn out all of the lights except for the Christmas tree. They will sit, snuggle, and talk for hours. . . . And they usually wind up bringing sleeping bags and pillows in so that they can sleep in front of the fire all night long!

CHRISTMAS COUNTDOWN

• • • • • • • • • • • • • •

When do you need to get your turkey
out to thaw? If you thaw it at room
temperature, place it in the sink in
cold water and allow 5 hours thawing
time per pound. Or figure 2—3 days
to thaw it in the refrigerator.

*"Through Jesus'
righteousness
the free gift of God
came to everyone—
freedom from guilt
and everlasting life."*

Romans 5:18

DECEMBER 23

We've all heard the story about the wise men coming to see Baby Jesus. We picture them riding across the desert on dark, still nights. Of course, they are on camels, passing oases of palm trees, and always, always keeping the star in view straight ahead of them. After a long, hard journey, they finally arrive in Bethlehem and fall to their knees in worship of the Christ Child, presenting their gifts of gold, frankincense, and myrrh. But if we look a little more closely at the *whole* story, we see that the wise men are also great examples of people who stand for what they believe no matter what anyone else says, does, or thinks.

The wise men had been going about their lives as usual, when suddenly one night, a star appeared that they had never seen before. Deciding that the star was a heavenly proclamation that a king had been born, the wise men did something no one else had ever done before. They followed a star in hopes of finding this new king so that they could worship him. Were they laughed at? Did their friends think they were a little crazy? There is no way to know for certain, but we do know that no one else came with them.

After they had traveled for many months, they arrived at Jerusalem. Surely the capital city is where the new king had been born! But they found the city in an uproar over their arrival! King Herod was filled with jealousy and rage over the possibility of someone trying to usurp his throne. The priests were busy searching the Scriptures to find out where the Messiah would be born. Housewives discussed the possibility of a new king as the bargained in the marketplace. "Has the Messiah really come?" they wondered. Workmen, worried about the wrath of Rome, asked "Will Caesar send more soldiers to crush any rumors of a new king and a possible rebellion?" And everyone gossiped about the magnificent wealth that accompanied these royal visitors from faraway lands. But in spite of the city's curiosity, none of those people came with the wise men to Bethlehem either.

Have you ever heard of peer pressure? Peer pressure is doing what everyone else is doing—even if it isn't the right thing to do or if it's something you don't want to do. No one likes to stand out in a group; no one wants to be the only one who stands against the crowd and points out what's right. We all want to be included.

But the wise men set out on a quest to find the King of kings. It involved setting aside what others thought and doing something totally different. God challenges us in the same way that He challenged the wise men. He asks each of us to follow Him completely. After all, finding the King of kings is the best adventure ever!

It has been said that a nation cannot chart its future if it does not have a thorough knowledge of its past. What is true of nations is also true of families . . . and it is true of individuals. Psalm 78:5-7 makes it clear that we have a responsibility to tell our children not only about the commandments of the Lord, but also about His works (see also Ex. 19:3; Ps. 48:13). We are to give them a sense of their own history and an awareness of God's personal interest in each of our lives; and there is no better way to do that than to share with them His mercies toward your family. The psalmist urges us to "declare what He has done for my soul!" (66:16) And the writer of Hebrews exhorts us to "encourage one another daily . . . lest any of you be hardened through the deceitfulness of sin" (3:13). Recounting the faithfulness of the Lord not only gives our children a sense of their own family history, but helps to establish them, protecting them from the influences of sin as they see God's mighty workings in *their* home.

One of my favorite ways to accomplish this is to take an hour or so and look through old photos. (This is an activity my children love.) This gives you an opportunity to share your family's history: your childhood, courtship, and marriage; funny things they did as preschoolers and the way they said words. Along with those stories, we tell them the stories of how we came to know the Lord, how He has provided for us, directed us, and protected us. Each of our children have faced life-threatening situations. We rehearse those stories—and remind them that it is the Lord who has sustained their lives! As they get older, they too join in, recounting things that the Lord has done for *them* personally: how they received Jesus as their Savior, how the Lord helped them in a difficult situation. They are familiarizing themselves with what God has done for them. As they do this, they will find it more and more difficult, even impossible, to deny God's existence—because they have already seen Him at work in their lives!

We also tell our children about the Lord's workings as we answer questions. One of our sons asked us recently about prayer and how it is answered. Not only were we able to teach him something new about life in the Lord, but we were also able to share with him ways that the Lord has answered us.

But perhaps the best way to make children aware of God's personal workings toward each of us is to let a spirit of thanksgiving permeate your home. As our children see us continually praising the Lord for the many blessings He pours out each day, they will begin to recognize His workings in each of their lives as well. What a solid foundation we are privileged to provide for our children of instruction, love, security, acceptance, and knowledge of the Lord!

CHRISTMAS COUNTDOWN

• • • • • • • • • • • • • •

Assemble and hide all large gifts. Maybe
a neighbor could help out here. One year
we refinished a bed for our daughter and
simply declared the garage off limits for
the month of December by posting a
large sign that read, "Santa's Workshop."

"Sin pays . . .
except it pays in death.
But God's gift is
life forever with Him
because of what
Jesus did for us
on the cross."

Romans 6:23

DECEMBER 24

The first verse that most of us ever memorize is John 3:16. Do you know it? Let's say it together:

> For God so loved 💚 the world that He gave His only begotten Son, that whoever believes in Him should not perish but have everlasting life. 🪙

Christmas is a gift giving and gift receiving time. But it's important to remember that we give gifts for a reason. It's a reminder that God gave us the greatest gift of all when He sent Jesus.

When Jesus enters our lives, not only do we receive God's gift, but we start to become like Him! That means that we become gift-givers too! We can be gift-givers by telling people about Jesus. We can be gift-givers by loving people and being kind. But at Christmas, we also get to be gift-givers by giving presents. Isn't it fun to go shopping and pick out the perfect gift for Mom and Dad? Or maybe you made something really special at school. Wrapping up the present, then waiting for Christmas morning to arrive is so exciting! I've wondered if that isn't the same kind of excitement God feels when we receive His gifts!

The Bible tells us that God is still giving us gifts! He not only gave us Jesus, but He gives us salvation, health, our special talents and abilities, the Bible, our family, and friends. 📖 James 1:17 says that, "Every good gift and every perfect gift is from above, and comes down from the Father." That means that every good thing that we have comes to us from God.

But when we become gift-givers, it involves one more thing. In the Christmas story, we read that the wise men brought Jesus gifts. We all know about the gold, frankincense, and myrrh. Those are some awesome gifts, but most of us don't have any of those things. However, the Bible also says that the wise men worshiped Jesus. That's something I can give Jesus! 🤍 The Bible teaches us that when we give the Lord our praise and thanksgiving, we are giving an offering to Him.

Let's do that this Christmas! If we remember that God was the very first gift-giver, opening presents around the Christmas tree will be a time of thankful-ness—not just for the presents 🎁 we receive, but for Jesus too.

Angels, from the Realms of Glory

REGENT SQUARE

James Montgomery

Henry Smart

1. An - gels, from the realms of glo - ry, Wing your flight o'er
2. Shep - herds, in the fields a - bid - ing, Watch - ing o'er your
3. Sag - es, leave your con - tem - pla - tions, Bright - er vi - sions
4. Saints, be - fore the al - tar bend - ing, Watch - ing long in

all the earth; Ye who sang cre - a - tion's sto - ry,
flocks by night, God with man is now re - sid - ing,
beam a - far; Seek the great De - sire of na - tions'
hope and fear, Sud - den - ly the Lord, de - scend - ing,

Now pro - claim Mes - si - ah's birth: Come and wor - ship,
Yon - der shines the in - fant Light: Come and wor - ship,
Ye have seen His na - tal star: Come and wor - ship,
In His tem - ple shall ap - pear; Come and wor - ship,

come and wor - ship, Wor - ship Christ, the new - born King!
come and wor - ship, Wor - ship Christ, the new - born King!
come and wor - ship, Wor - ship Christ, the new - born King!
come and wor - ship, Wor - ship Christ, the new - born King!

When it comes time to wrap gifts, take all of the gift wrapping supplies in by the children. Not only will you enjoy the time together, but children *love* to wrap gifts and they can help a lot. They can find boxes, stick on bows, and hand you pieces of tape. And you *always* need an extra person to hold everything secure while you tie the string! My children also enjoy choosing which paper will go on whose gift.

Something we've done is to wrap gifts in themes. Once we wrapped everything with solid red paper and white ribbon. Sometimes we will wrap gifts by families: one kind of paper for all the gifts that go to Uncle Jack and Aunt Joann's family, another kind for Uncle Dennis and Aunt Cathy's family. One year we were so broke that we wrapped everything in plain brown paper tied with red and green yarn. Then for bows, the children stuck on bright colored leaves out of our yard!

Another thing that we've enjoyed doing is decorating the outside of the boxes we mail. One year we bought different colored dot-stickers from the office supply store and stuck them all over the boxes. Then the children drew happy faces on all the dots. But usually I give them a supply of Christmas stickers and red and green markers. (Just be sure to leave the address space clear!)

Of course, wrapping gifts with the children doesn't work when it comes to their gifts. For their presents, I try to get all of the shopping and wrapping done before school is out. If you have responsibilities during the day, try my all time favorite December "get-my-head-together-I-need-some-space-too" alone time. I'll wait until everyone is asleep, turn on some of my favorite music, and wrap gifts all by myself!

And when they see their gifts all wrapped and ready, does *that* ever intensify the excitement!

CHRISTMAS COUNTDOWN

• • • • • • • • • • • • • • • •

Are you ready for the big day tomorrow?
Today is the day to make ahead any food
possible. Bake pies, prepare any dishes
that can be refrigerated, get your stuffing
mixed (but don't stuff the turkey until
right before you put it in the oven), and
take out any frozen dishes that you made
earlier in the month.

"*When the*
wise men had come . . .
they gave gifts
to the Child Jesus:
gold, frankincense,
and myrrh."

Matthew 2:11

DECEMBER 25

These are the facts concerning the birth of Jesus Christ:

Before anything else existed, there was Christ, with God. And Christ became a human being and lived here on earth among us and was full of loving forgiveness and truth. And some of us have seen His glory—the glory of the only Son of the Heavenly Father.

∞ ∞ ∞

His mother, Mary, was engaged to be married to Joseph. But while she was still a virgin she became pregnant by the Holy Spirit.

[The Angel] Gabriel appeared to her and said, "Don't be frightened, Mary, for God has decided to wonderfully bless you! Very soon now, you will become pregnant and have a baby boy, and you are to name Him 'Jesus.' He shall be very great and shall be called the Son of God. And the Lord God shall give Him the throne of His ancestor David. And He shall reign over Israel forever; His kingdom shall never end!"

Mary asked the angel, "But how can I have a baby? I am a virgin."

The angel replied, "The Holy Spirit shall come upon you, and the power of God shall overshadow you; so the baby born to you will be utterly holy—the Son of God."

Mary said, "I am the Lord's servant, and I am willing to do whatever He wants. May everything you said come true." And then the angel disappeared.

Then Joseph, her fiance, being a man of stern principle, decided to break the engagement but to do it quietly, as he didn't want to publicly disgrace her. As he lay awake considering this, he fell into a dream, and saw an angel standing beside him. "Joseph, son of David," the angel said, "don't hesitate to take Mary as your wife! For the child within her has been conceived by the Holy Spirit. And she will have a Son, and you shall name Him Jesus (meaning 'Savior'), for He will save His people from their sins. This will fulfill God's message through His prophets—

'Listen! The virgin shall conceive a child! She shall give birth to a Son, and He shall be called "Emmanuel" (meaning "God is with us").'"

When Joseph awoke, he did as the angel commanded.

∞ ∞ ∞

About this time Caesar Augustus, the Roman Emperor, ordered that a census should be taken. Everyone was required to return to his ancestral home for this registration. And because Joseph was a member of the royal line, he had to go to Bethlehem in Judea, King David's ancient home—journeying there from the Galilean village of Nazareth. He took with him Mary, his fiancee, who was obviously pregnant by this time.

And while they were there, the time came for her baby to be born, and she gave birth to her first child, a son. She wrapped Him in a blanket and laid Him in a manger, because there was no room for them in the village inn.

That night some shepherds were in the fields outside the village, guarding their flocks of sheep. Suddenly an angel appeared among them, and the countryside shone bright with the glory of the Lord.

"Don't be afraid!" the angel said. "I bring you the most joyful news ever announced, and it is for everyone! The Savior—yes, the Messiah, the Lord—has been born tonight in Bethlehem! How will you recognize Him? You will find a baby wrapped in a blanket, lying in a manger!"

Suddenly, the angel was joined by a huge host of other angels—the armies of heaven—praising God:

"Glory to God in the highest heaven," they sang, "and on earth, peace to all men."

When this great army of angels had returned again to heaven, the shepherds said to each other, "Come on! Let's go to Bethlehem! Let's see this wonderful thing that has happened, which the Lord has told us about."

They ran to the village and found Mary and Joseph. And there was the baby, lying in the manger. Then the shepherds went back again to their fields and flocks, praising God for the visit of the angels, and because they had seen the child, just as the angel had told them.

At about that time some wise men from eastern lands arrived in Jerusalem, asking, "Where is the newborn King of the Jews? We have seen His star and have come to worship Him."

King Herod was deeply disturbed by their question, and all Jerusalem was filled with rumors. He called a meeting of the Jewish religious leaders.

"Did the prophets tell us where the Messiah would be born?" he asked.

"Yes, in Bethlehem," they said, "for this is what the Prophet Micah wrote:

'O little town of Bethlehem, you are not just an unimportant Judean village, for a Ruler shall rise from you to rule My people Israel.'"

Then Herod sent a private message to the wise men. He told them, "Go to Bethlehem and search for the child. And when you find Him, come back and tell me so that I can go and worship Him too!"

After this interview the wise men started out again. And look! The star appeared to them again, standing over Bethlehem. Their joy knew no bounds!

Entering the house where the baby and Mary His mother were, they threw themselves down before Him, worshiping. Then they opened their presents and gave Him gold, frankincense and myrrh.

Eight days later, at the baby's circumcision ceremony, He was named Jesus, the name given Him by the angel before He was even conceived.

℘ ℘ ℘

God gave Him a name which is above every other name, that at the name of Jesus every knee shall bow in heaven and on earth and under the earth, and every tongue shall confess that Jesus Christ is Lord, to the glory of God the Father.

excerpted from *The Living Bible*
Matthew 1, 2
Luke 1, 2
John 1
Philippians 2

Good Christian Men, Rejoice

Latin, 14th Century
Tr. by John M. Neale

IN DULCI JUBILO
14th Century German Melody

1. Good Chris-tian men, re - joice__ With heart and soul and voice!__
2. Good Chris-tian men, re - joice__ With heart and soul and voice!__
3. Good Chris-tian men, re - joice__ With heart and soul and voice!__

Give ye heed to what we say: Je - sus Christ is born to - day.
Now ye hear of end - less bliss: Je - sus Christ was born for this.
Now ye need not fear the grave: Je - sus Christ was born to save;

Man and beast be - fore Him bow, And He is in the man-ger now:
He hath o - pened heav-en's door, And man is blessed for - ev - er-more.
Calls you one, and calls you all, To gain His ev - er - last - ing hall.

Christ is born to - day,_____ Christ is born to - day!__
Christ was born for this,_____ Christ was born for this!__
Christ was born to save,_____ Christ was born to save!__

Christmas morning is usually so full of activity that I try to keep breakfast *simple*; yet Christmas is also a special day and so I want to have something *special*. But "special" is basically anything we don't usually have. Our Christmas morning breakfasts have ranged from the super simple—like doughnuts and hot chocolate, to the more involved with quiche, muffins, and fruit salad, to our oldest son making blueberry waffles for everyone with one of his latest Christmas gifts: a Snoopy waffle iron! Here are some ideas to keep your morning meal simple AND special.

For Christmas morning breakfast, make sure that you've done all of your menu planning and grocery shopping by December 22. This allows you to make as much as possible ahead of time on December 23. The year we served quiche, we had 2 dozen relatives at our house—that's a lot of quiche! But we made the quiches about a week ahead and froze them. Then on Christmas morning, they just went into the oven while we opened gifts. Simple—yet special!

Other easy or make ahead breakfasts are waffles (either homemade or the pop-in-the-toaster type), pie (I claim that these are no different than fruit-filled pastries), or cereal (let the kids pick something just for fun).

Some families don't like standard breakfast fare. If this is the case with your family, try something like a pizza, but shape the crust like a Christmas tree. Vegetable-filled omelets or turkey and cranberry sauce sandwiches might also be workable suggestions for you.

Just remember that in the midst of making things "special," don't lose the "simple." Enjoy your breakfast . . . and let the holiday begin!

CHRISTMAS COUNTDOWN
• • • • • • • • • •

You've seen pictures in magazines; you've seen it on TV; you've read hints in the paper on how to roast those tender, succulent, juicy turkeys that melt in your mouth! So why is accomplishing this in the privacy of our own homes so complicated for most of us?

The major reason we turn out dry turkey after dry turkey, is that we remember Grandma roasting her turkeys for hours and hours—all night in fact! The difference is that with modern poultry raising techniques, turkeys don't need to roast forever to become tender. In fact, they need to roast less to stay juicy! The following chart will give you a good idea of how long to roast your turkey.

TIME TABLE FOR ROASTING

	Oven temp.	Minutes per pound
	325°	
Under 8 pounds		25-30
8-16 pounds		20-25
Over 16 pounds		No more than 7 hrs. total

CHRISTMAS COUNTDOWN
● ● ● ● ● ● ● ● ● ● ● ● ●

The week between Christmas and New Year's Day tends to be a "lost" week for many people. Very few things are scheduled for this week, and our tendency is to lay around and gaze in dismay at our dried-up Christmas trees and punch-stained carpets!

One year, however, I decided to redeem this last week of December so that our family could begin the new year with a "clean slate."

Here's what we do:

1. Undecorate the house. When I do this, I repair or clean up anything that needs it so I don't have to mess with it during a busy next December.

2. Evaluate how everything went this year. Write down whatever comes to mind that would make the holidays go more smoothly next year. This could be as simple as remembering to buy more ice, or as involved as planning an open house.

3. Find places to put away all of the gifts. This is a project in itself— especially with the kids' stuff! We get this out of the way during this week, and at the same time I try to get the children's closets straightened up (again!).

4. Write your thank-you notes. After the New Year when everything is back in full swing, you won't feel like it!

5. Enjoy your family. This week generally doesn't require much of anybody, so we spend time together. In fact, my husband tries to arrange a few vacation days during this time . . . and that makes it even better!

6. Spend time with the Lord. At the end of each year, I like to spend some time talking to Jesus about the past year and what He wants my vision and goals to be for the coming year. I write all of these down in a letter to Him and review it a year later. It's amazing to watch how He answers and brings things to fulfillment from losing that 5 pounds gained during December to the salvation of a dear friend. Present all of those things to Him! And as you do, it is my prayer that this book will continue to be a blessing to your family for many Christmases to come

. . . and happy new year!